PORTRAIT OF ESSEX

Broadland Naturalist
The Right Way to Understand the Countryside
A Ladybird Book of Butterflies, Moths and other Insects
Trees and Forests
Bakers and Bread
Systematic Guide to Flowering Plants of the World
The Insect World
The Woodland World
The Naturalist in South-East England (Kent, Surrey and
    Sussex)
Nature in East Anglia (Norfolk and Suffolk)

Portrait of
ESSEX

S. A. MANNING

Photographs by Richard Jemmett

ROBERT HALE · LONDON

© *S. A. Manning 1977*
First published in Great Britain 1977

ISBN 0 7091 6388 6

Robert Hale Limited
Clerkenwell House
Clerkenwell Green
London EC1R 0HT

PRINTED IN GREAT BRITAIN BY
LOWE & BRYDONE LTD., THETFORD
PHOTOSET AND BOUND BY
WEATHERBY WOOLNOUGH, WELLINGBOROUGH

To the memory of my wife,
Rosemary Dinah Manning (1929-1976),
dedicated nurse and woman of conscience,
who loved Essex and the English countryside.

CONTENTS

I	The Essex Scene	11
II	The Essex Coast	33
III	The Rivers	51
IV	The Great County Towns	69
V	Towns, Villages and Churches	83
VI	The New Towns	98
VII	The Good Earth	116
VIII	Industry	134
IX	Nature in Essex	148
X	Cultural and Leisure Activities	167
	Index	180

ILLUSTRATIONS

Between pages 48 and 49

Arable farming at Wix
Wheatfields near Bradfield
Billericay: the Chequers Inn
Town Hall, Harlow New Town
Basildon
West Stockwell Street, Colchester
Chelmsford: the cathedral
The River Chelmer, near Little Baddow

Between pages 96 and 97

Saffron Walden: an ancient corner
In Epping Forest
The pier-end at Southend-on-Sea
White Street at Great Dunmow
Swans beside the River Stour at Mistley
Tower mill at Stansted Mountfitchet
Courtauld's factory at Halstead
New industrial estate at Halstead
Yardley factory at Basildon
New town skyline at Basildon

Between pages 144 and 145

Colchester Castle
Chelmsford, the shopping centre
Coastal erosion at Walton-on-the-Naze
Coast protection at Walton-on-the-Naze

Headquarters of the Essex Naturalists Trust, Fingringhoe
   Wick
Swans, shipping and maltings at Mistley
Funfair and pier at Clacton-on-Sea
The busy port of Harwich
The church and inn at Great Waltham
Churchend and church of St Mary, Great Dunmow
Town Street from the ancient guildhall, Thaxted
Chapel Street, Billericay
Cereal crops near Thaxted
Harvesting beans at Saffron Walden
All Saints' Church, Stock
All Saints' Church, Norton Mandeville

PICTURE CREDITS

All photographs by Richard Jemmett

MAP   *Pages 178-179*

I

THE ESSEX SCENE

ESSEX is a county of stimulating contrasts, of hills and level marshland, of factory and farm, of moated mansion and modern tower-block, of computer-minded businessman and handworking craftsman. One could make the list much longer! To many people the surprising thing is that, despite the construction of bold new roads and the mechanization of transport, agriculture and various other everyday activities, there are still places where it is possible to experience a sense of what life was like in centuries long ago.

The variety of scene is something for which many visitors are completely unprepared, largely because variation in contour and landscape is often subtle and missed by the motorist with his eye on the road. Yet even a cursory glance at a chart of the county's structural features reveals and explains much. Rising to just under 500 feet, the highest ground of all is in the extreme north-western corner, an area of flattened chalk hills where fine views across rolling country are gained through gaps in tall hedges festooned with old man's beard or traveller's joy, a wild clematis.

Beyond the highest ground the larger north-western sector consists of irregular spreading ridges. More of these tongues of higher land occur in the south-western quarter of the county – Epping Forest Ridge, Brentwood-Norton Heath Ridge, Highwood Ridge, Thorndon-Billericay-Galleywood Ridge, and a few others. The northern and southern ridges descend to lower plateaus whose rugged edges push into the lower eastern side of Essex. But even in this lower region the Tiptree and Danbury Ridges and the Langdon, Dengie and Rayleigh Hills create diversity and surprise in a county which, for generations, has been misrepresented as 'flat' and also as 'an utter abomination of desolation' (the latter words

11

summarized certain opinions in 1901).

Farmers and others who are intimately concerned with such details realize only too well that soil types and textures are also subject to much variation throughout Essex. Light and medium soils – sands, gravels, chalk and loams occur, and heavier clays are widespread in many parts. Alluvial soils are more abundant, particularly around the coast, in the southern half of the county, though they are by no means absent in the north.

Chalk, occurring near the surface in both the north and the south, has proved to be a useful material in the county. Clunch from hard bands in the chalk has been used for building and also for ornamentation. Although it is not always regarded as being completely weather-resistant, clunch has not been confined to interior work. Much use of this material was made in the construction of St Mary's at Saffron Walden. Cottages, too, have been made of clunch at places like Great Chesterford and Hempstead in the north of Essex.

Extensive use has been made in Essex buildings of flint, the very hard steel-grey stone whose irregularly-shaped lumps are found in the upper levels of the chalk and in chalky boulder clay. Sometimes, as at Hedingham and Saffron Walden castles, flint rubble formed the core of massive thick walls, stone for use as facing occasionally being brought in from other counties. Elsewhere flint appears as a building material in its own right, exposed to view without facing. The fourteenth-century St Nicholas' at Witham is a 'flint church' and in the same town the nineteenth-century builders of All Saints' church made use of flint and white brick.

Perhaps the most pleasing and effective use of flint is in knapped flint and flushwork decoration, work for which East Anglia has long been renowned. There is a fine example of such work at Colchester, where the fifteenth-century gatehouse of St John's Abbey on St John's Green displays, at least to the outside world, much decorative use of flint. Rather than refer to what a contemporary writer has called its 'much patched-up state,' one reflects that this ancient structure has survived the dissolution of the monasteries, the siege of Colchester, nineteenth-century restoration and two world wars. The fifteenth-century gatehouse of St Osyth Abbey displays a magnificent façade to passers-by and, here again, this is largely due to the beautifully executed flushwork panelling. From the quatrefoil frieze at the base to the chequer-pattern of the battlements, with its alternate squares of cut flint and stone, all elements in the design blend together, creating a natural wholeness.

A certain amount of flint appears in the fabric of the parish church of St Peter and St Paul at St Osyth. Here, too, use was made of septaria in, for example, the facing of the north aisle. Septaria is found mainly in the northeast of the county in the London clays as hardish lumps whose cracks, the septa from which the material takes its name, are filled with mineral calc-spar or pyrites. Light reddish yellow ('ginger') to orange-yellow in colour, septaria has added variety to the colour and texture of buildings in many parts of Essex. There is septaria in the walls of St Botolph's Priory, whose ruins stand in Colchester, and this concretionary form of clay was included, together with Roman bricks and dressed stones, in the nearby castle keep where the well, over forty feet deep, is lined with it.

Two of the building materials already mentioned, flint and septaria, are used in the tower of Lawford church, as are brick and pudding stone. The last-named was obviously given its name because, as a conglomerate, it somewhat resembles a fruit pudding, pebbles taking the place of currants or raisins. Sometimes rust stained from the presence of ironstone, pudding stone brings colour to walls and towers. The Norman tower of St Peter's church at Boxted is of this rough material. Pebble rubble was also commonly used by the builders of many Essex churches, including those at Chrishall, Clavering and Thaxted.

With so much of this material available in the area, it is not surprising that clay should have been mixed with straw and moulded into clay lump. The dried blocks produced in this way were, in effect, unfired bricks. With a protective coating of lime plaster, they were used in the construction of cottages and farm buildings. Many such structures of clay lump have disappeared but occasionally one comes across them in places off the beaten track.

The Romans built with unfired-clay blocks on stone footings, but went further and fired clay to produce their own bricks, which were usually less hard than modern ones. In Essex large numbers of Roman bricks found their way into later castles and churches. The church of St Peter's by the sea-wall at Bradwell, the earliest Saxon building (about 654) to survive in the county, is almost entirely built of Roman brick and other Roman materials. At Holy Trinity church, Colchester, there are Roman bricks in the west tower, the only Anglo-Saxon building left in the town. Here, too, Roman bricks were used in the construction of the early-Norman church of St Botolph's Priory and the Norman castle, where they appear in the rubble core of the walls of the keep and also in an internal wall. There are more examples of Norman work with Roman bricks in other parts of the county and it has been calculated that at least 103 Essex churches embody re-used Roman material.

Brickmaking is generally thought to have died out with the Romans, being reintroduced from the continent early in the thirteenth-century. Be this as it may, there is little doubt that red bricks used at Little Coggeshall Abbey, whose foundation dates from about 1140 (it was made Cistercian in 1148), are examples of the thirteenth century. There are other early-medieval bricks, specimens of a date no later than 1300, in the fabric of the remarkable Norman parish church of St Mary the Virgin at Copford.

As the years passed brick was increasingly employed in both ecclesiastical and domestic architecture. At Ingatestone the west tower of the church of St Edmund and St Mary is a magnificent example of the use of red brick with black diapers, while at Layer Marney (site of the famous Towers, a tall early sixteenth-century red-brick gatehouse, which brought the Renaissance into Essex) the sixteenth-century church of St Mary the Virgin is also of red brick but with blue diapering. The brick tower, red with blue diapering, of St Mary's church at Gestingthorpe, a village with its own brickfield until early this century, is of about 1498. An inscription on the west face of the red-brick tower of St Nicholas church at Castle Hedingham states that it was renovated in 1616, which emphasizes that it is of even earlier date. And so one could continue for some time about the use of that beautiful and convenient building material in the churches of Essex.

As one turns to the use of brick in secular architecture, one feels that it is a great pity that so little seems to be known about the brickmakers and the builders. Perhaps we must be content with the buildings themselves, compensating for our lack of information by showing genuine appreciation of present-day craftsmen and offering them real support whenever possible.

Faulkbourne Hall provides an impressive example of the early use of brick in domestic dwellings, though the castle-like appearance of part of it suggests a less-peaceful use. It was after 1439, when Sir John Montgomery, a distinguished soldier, was permitted to crenellate his house, that brick parts began to be added to the original timber-framed house. Now the hall includes brickwork from the fifteenth century down to much more recent times. Horham Hall, Thaxted, is another of the county's fine, early brick mansions. This house, unfinished when its builder, Sir John Cutte, Henry VIII's Treasurer of the Household, died in 1520, is noteworthy not only for its early sixteenth-century red brick but also for the splendid mullioned window and lantern of its Great Hall. Horham Hall was, by the way, one of more than a score of Essex houses visited by Elizabeth I during her progresses through these parts. She was here in 1571 and again in 1578 during the time of a later Sir John Cutte, a most extravagant man at whose death the house passed from the family. Equally interesting stories could be told of many more of the county's older brick buildings, details of which should be sought in Pevsner's *Essex* volume in *The Buildings of England* series.

In a county once extensively covered with forest, it is only to be expected that wood forms a large or important part of many old buildings that survive here. Mention is made elsewhere in this book of the famous log-church of St Andrew at Greensted and of the recent scientific tests whose results suggest a date of about 835 for most of the nave timbers and an even earlier date for some of them. As the only surviving medieval English timber church, St Andrew's is unique in both county and country.

Unique as it is, it is but part of a great heritage of buildings in which timber is the main material. Most of the sixty-five timber-framed belfries were built, with considerable skill in design and construction, in the southern half of Essex. That at West Hanningfield has a unique cruciform plan. One expert believes that it is thirteenth-century, but it has also been suggested that it is later than this. Whatever its date, its internal construction of arched braces and buttressing struts reflects great credit on its designer and builder (probably, in those days, one and the same person). Navestock belfry is one of a group whose members are outside the west end of the church. This particular tower is carried on four heavy posts to which shafts carrying arched braces are attached towards the centre. The results of radiocarbon tests on the Navestock timbers suggest that the wood used dates from the twelfth or thirteenth century, but there are reasons for thinking that the belfry was erected some time before 1250. Certainly it is known to have contained two bells in 1297. The belfry of Mount-nessing church is an example of the type that is built within the western end of the nave. An impressive arrangement of six posts, cross beams, braces and buttressing struts, it stands as an independent structure.

Timber-framed houses are another important part of the county's great heritage. Many of them have been altered and some almost disguised over the years but, even so, their great number and variety of form add considerably to the interest of the Essex scene. Chelmsford, the county town, has its share of timber-framed cottages, particularly in Moulsham Street. Colchester, too, is well worth exploring, but one must be ready to seek out its timbered treasures on foot and at leisure.

The Red Lion Hotel in High Street is a timber-framed building of the late fifteenth century with projecting upper storeys and exposed front timbers. Visitors who are tempted to sample the fare provided will be rewarded in more ways than one, for moulded beams and carved brackets are still to be seen inside this old inn. In East Street, site of a medieval suburb, the fifteenth-century Siege House has its timber framing marked by bullets fired during the Siege of 1648. Nearby is another carefully restored old building, the large timber-framed Rose and Crown Hotel. Down North Hill are fifteenth-century timber-framed houses and the early sixteenth-century Marquis of Granby Inn, with its restored half-timbered front and richly-carved interior work. There are other timbered houses of interest in West Stockwell Street and its neighbourhood. There is not sufficient space to catalogue those existing in the countryside. I can only urge the reader to get out and about, seeking them for himself, always remembering that each old house is someone's home and may also be the centre of a busy farm.

This last word serves to remind one of the splendid timber-framed barns that add to the county's heritage and character. Two of the most magnificent examples stand at Cressing where the Templars, the military order of knights, sergeants and chaplains, settled in the twelfth century, including farming among their activities, and where, on their suppression by Pope Clement V, the Hospitallers, the military order of the knights or brethren of the hospital of St John at Jerusalem, replaced them in 1312. The barley barn is weather-boarded, the wheat barn brick nogged, the spaces between the studs (the timbers) being filled with bricks. Both these pre-1330 barns are aisled. The wheat barn, the larger of the two is 140 feet long and 40 feet high. Some massive timbers were needed in their construction, whole oaks being used as main posts. There are other old barns at Little Coggeshall, High Roding, Belchamp St Paul, and near Felsted.

Moated sites outnumber ancient timber-framed barns in the county. This is not surprising because Essex, with almost 800, contains the highest number of recorded moated sites for any county. Very little is known about most of them, though many are believed to have been constructed between the twelfth and fourteenth centuries. Various reasons have been advanced for the excavation of moats. The wide ditch served, it is argued, to drain the site, the house being built on the land, often raised, in the moated enclosure. Defence against marauders, human and animal, was ensured, and the moat could be used as an important source of water, fish and even waterfowl. But there are people who think that these suggestions are somewhat naïve, and that only too often a moat was a status symbol, a way of keeping up with one's superiors in the social order. We will not argue about this, but we can be sure that moats do add to the interest of places and that they can form useful little reserves for wild life. A number of moated houses (or their grounds) may be visited on occasion. In hesitating to name them, because arrangements vary so much from year to year, one urges readers to watch local newspapers for announcements and to obtain the various lists that are issued of houses and gardens open to the public. And, of course, one feels obliged to add a gentle and courteous reminder that any conditions imposed by owners should be carefully and willingly observed.

In setting out to explore the Essex countryside itself, whether as walker, rider or motorist, the reader will appreciate that, while he has the right to use public roads and rights of way, he also has a duty to respect the privacy and livelihood of those who live in the country. The great contribution made by those who live by the land is dealt with in some detail elsewhere in this book. Nowadays, farmers, foresters and others have it within their power, so far as laws and regulations allow, to change the appearance of their localities far more easily and quickly than ever before. This is an aspect of modern life that can produce some unpleasant effects – the uprooting of hedgerows and the erection of pylons in places where scenic beauty is thereby destroyed, to quote but two examples. Nevertheless these are but incidents in the long history of man, a history of which it is not always easy to find evidence.

In prehistoric times there was little human settlement in Essex, then a densely wooded area. However, one of the earliest-known occupied sites in Britain is in the county, at Clacton, type-site for the Clactonian culture. These people arrived at the beginning of the second glaciation, 475-450,000 years ago, and used anvil-stones to make rough choppers, heavy scrapers, various kinds of points, and core-tools from flints. Much later, during the Mesolithic period (about 12,000 to 3,000 BC), two main groups were active here, Maglemosians with their bone implements and axes and other products of the flint industry, and Sauveterrians with small flint blades (microliths). These primitive peoples were wandering food-gatherers and hunters.

By the start of the Neolithic (New Stone Age), in about 4,000 BC, the first farmers had arrived from the continent. Besides influencing and interbreeding with the primitive folk they found here, these farmers introduced the very basis of our civilisation, our more settled way of life. An important and productive Neolithic site lies under the sea off Walton-on-the-Naze and examples of the carefully made flint tools are still washed ashore. There are specimens of Neolithic pottery from

Lawford in the Colchester and Essex Museum at Colchester.

With the introduction from Europe of copper tools and ornaments the Neolithic ended, giving way to the Early Bronze Age. By about 2,000 BC the Beaker peoples, named after their characteristic pots, arrived with knowledge of metal-working, at first in copper and later in tin-bronze, and with their own custom of burying their dead under round mounds (barrows). The important collections at the Colchester and Essex Museum include several finds representative of the Early Bronze Age – 'beakers' from sites in north-east Essex, a group of gold and amber beads from Rochford, and axes. Among finds from the Middle Bronze Age, when people were settling on the higher lands, are urns from cemeteries at Ardleigh and White Colne, and axes and bronze spearheads. Improved axes, swords and hoards of scrap bronze from the Late Bronze Age have also been found in the county.

The Early Iron Age began when iron was introduced from about 700 BC by settlers from the continent. At Linford, in the extreme south of Essex, excavation has been undertaken at the site of a small farmstead of the fourth century BC, the period towards the end of Iron Age A, and there are a few finds of this culture from Witham and Kelvedon. The La Tene (Iron Age B) culture had a certain influence in Essex, but it was the Iron Age C peoples, the vigorous and able Belgae, who arrived here from about 150 BC, who really made their presence felt. They used the heavy plough with share, struck their own coins, made pottery on the wheel, produced fine metalwork, and traded with the Roman Empire, importing Roman objects. Some idea of their advanced state of culture can be gained from the rich Iron-Age collections in the Colchester and Essex Museum, where the displays include bronzes, armour, cere-monial furniture and other finds from the Lexden tumulus, the great burial mound in Colchester, and pottery.

At the time of Julius Caesar's expedition of 55 BC, when the Romans invaded Britain, showed their power and tested the strength of the natives, the inhabitants of Essex, the Trinovantes, were at war with the Catuvellauni, their western neighbours. Evidence of these uneasy times is seen in the surviving remains of Iron-Age hill-forts and camps. In Epping Forest there are two such sites. Loughton Camp, with its single

rampart and forty-five-foot wide ditch, covers 6½ acres on a
spur one mile north-west of St Mary's church, while at
Ambresbury Banks, 2¾ miles south of Epping Upland church,
are the rampart and ditch of a hill-fort covering about twelve
acres. Also on the western edge of Essex, Wallbury Camp, on a
spur 1½ miles south-west of Great Hallingbury church, occupies
some thirty-one acres. Like the Iron-Age encampment at
Pitchbury Ramparts, two miles south of Great Horkesley
church, it was defended by a wide ditch and a double rampart,
the latter being an unusual feature. In the north-west of the
county, facing Audley End mansion, 1½ miles west of Saffron
Walden, the Iron-Age hill-fort of Ring Hill has within its
ramparts an Ionic temple. This was built in 1770-2 to com-
memorate the ending of the Seven Years War by the Treaty of
Paris of 1763. Truly a spot with widely separated historical
associations!

During his brief visit, Caesar is reputed to have imposed
an uneasy peace. Uneasy is the word, for eventually the
Trinovantes of Essex were conquered by the Catuvellauni
whose ruler, Cunobelin, greatest of the Belgic kings, seized
Camulodunum (Colchester) about AD 5-10 and established his
capital there. Cunobelin died in AD 40 or 41 and was succeeded
by his sons Caratacus and Togodumnus, young men who are
said to have had no sense of restraint or of diplomatic moder-
ation. Meanwhile, the Romans were concerned about the
defence of the coast of Gaul, point of departure of refugees
leaving for Britain and of arrival of raiders and others from
that country. They also had knowledge of British trading with
the continent, of Britain's mineral wealth and manpower, and
of the existence in the country of Druidism, the religion they
were suppressing in Gaul.

In AD 43 the Roman Conquest of Britain was begun and
the defeat of Caratacus at the battle of the Medway allowed
the triumphant entry of the Emperor Claudius into
Camulodunum (Colchester). This ancient town is the subject
of part of a later chapter, but one hopes that the reader, if he
has not already done so, will visit Colchester, inspect the
Roman walls and the great collections of finds from the
Roman town in the Colchester and Essex Museum, including
the bronze statue of Mercury, which was ploughed up near the

temple at Gosbecks, military tombstones, glass, pottery, domestic objects, coins and tessellated and mosaic pavements. Such a survey is essential if one is to appreciate the advanced levels of culture and technical ability achieved by the Romans.

Colchester survived for about forty years after the Romans officially and finally separated Britain from their Empire in AD 410. Later the natives, never very keen on many of the Roman ways, had to contend with the arrival of Saxons. Unlike earlier Saxons, who arrived as mercenaries, raiders and pirates, these people, mostly lowland farmers, came as settlers. Saxon kingdoms were formed and our area became that of the East Saxons by the end of the sixth century.

In the closing years of the same century St Augustine, sent from Rome as a missionary, brought Christianity to this country. Mellitus, who had been sent from Rome to reinforce Augustine, was consecrated bishop in 604 and sent to preach to the East Saxons. After some initial success, there followed a short period of banishment and his eventual return to Kent and appointment as third Archbishop of Canterbury. In 653 St Cedd, who became bishop a year later, was sent from Northumbria to convert the East Saxons. He administered his diocese from Othona, now Bradwell-on-Sea, where the chapel he dedicated to St Peter in about 654 still stands, and from West Tilbury, where the hillside below the church has been suggested as the probable site of his church. Cedd died of plague at his monastery at Lastingham in Yorkshire in 664. A number of his followers died of the same disease and it is recorded that many converted East Saxons, fearing that the old gods were taking their revenge, reverted to paganism.

By the beginning of the seventh century London and Middlesex were included in the Kingdom of the East Saxons, but both seem to have been lost during the following century to Mercia, whose control of Essex extended into part of the ninth century. The defeat of Mercia by Wessex at the battle of Ellandune in 825 led to the incorporation of Essex (and certain other parts of England) into the kingdom of the West Saxons. In the later ninth century Essex became part of the kingdom of Greater East Anglia established by the Danish army under Guthrum.

The Danes appear to have used Essex mainly as a base from which to raid other parts, but this often brought trouble to the area. Such was the case when, after their return from an unsuccessful attack on Kent, the Danes seized Mersea Island and built a fort at Benfleet. At this last-named place they were overcome by the forces of Alfred the Great and their ships burnt, but Mersea Island and their fort at Shoebury remained to serve them as bases for further expeditions.

When Alfred's successor, his son King Edward the Elder, set about reconquering the Danish areas early in the tenth century, he made camp at Maldon, constructed a fort at Witham, where scant evidence of lines of entrenchment exists on Chippinghill, and in 917 expelled the Danish garrison from Colchester, afterwards repairing the town walls.

After the reconquest in 920, Essex became part of a united England. The majority of the population, Saxons and Danes alike, appear to have established a community of interest, regarding themselves as Englishmen. The kings of England came and went: Edward the Elder died, and his eldest son Athelstan reigned for fifteen years. Then came Edward the Elder's fifth son Edmund I, who bled to death from a wound six years after becoming king. His brother Edred died nine years after succeeding him. The three-year reign of Edmund's eldest son Edwy ended when he died of grief after trouble with Dunstan. This "turbulent and ambitious priest", later to become Saint Dunstan, apparently rebuked Edwy for leaving the coronation feast to visit a mistress! Edwy's brother, Edgar the Peaceable, king from 958 to 975, was disliked in certain quarters on account of his Danish sympathies. His son, Edward the Martyr, reigned for about three years before being murdered at the instance of his mother-in-law.

Edward was followed by his half-brother, Ethelred II, a weak king known to history as 'the unready', during whose reign a mint was established at Colchester. Danish raids were resumed soon after his accession in 979. In 991 a large force of Danish raiders, who attacked Ipswich from the sea before turning south into Essex, fought the battle of Maldon, defeated the English, and plundered and murdered throughout the district. Ethelred tried to buy off the Danish raiders by paying Danegeld, and then, on St Brice's Day, 1002, he ordered the massacre of the Danes settled in England. This provoked an invasion by Sweyn of Denmark in 1003, the first of several between then and 1013. Much Danish ravaging took place throughout the south and finally, in 1013, Ethelred fled the country, leaving Sweyn to be acknowledged as king of England.

Sweyn and Ethelred died in quick succession and, on 18th October, 1016, their sons, Cnut and Edmund Ironside, met in battle at Ashingdon, Essex, when the English were decisively defeated by the Danes, aided by the treachery of some of the English leaders. Within a month Edmund was dead and the following year Cnut was chosen king of England. He is reputed to have courted English favour by benefactions to monasteries, and there is a charming story of his Danish standard-bearer, Tofig (Tovi) the Proud, building at Waltham Holy Cross, where Harold's great abbey was consecrated in 1060, a shrine for a beautiful cross found through a vision on his estate at Montacute in Somerset.

From 1016 to 1042 Essex, like the rest of England, was under Danish rule, first of Cnut and then of his natural son Harold I and later of his son Hardacnut. The last-named, an extraordinary creature who is recorded as having disinterred and insulted the body of King Harold, died suddenly of repletion at a marriage feast, thus bringing the dynasty of Danish rulers of England to an end.

The year before he died Hardacnut had invited to court his half-brother Edward the Confessor who was crowned king of England in 1043. Edward entered the county's affairs when he attended the consecration of Waltham Abbey, but what was of much greater significance to Essex and the entire country (and even beyond that) was the visit to his court of William Duke of Normandy (afterwards William I) to whom, it is thought probable, the Confessor promised the kingdom.

Be this as it may, it is also said that, on his death-bed early in 1066, the Confessor had named as his successor Harold, son of Earl Godwin, a choice accepted by the nobles. The new king Harold II, whose memorial in Essex must surely be the remains of Waltham Abbey, had a few years earlier, when he was shipwrecked and taken to William, sworn on the relics to be the Duke of Normandy's man in England. William invaded England on Harold's accession and, with the English king's death after reigning for only nine months, became at the Battle

of Hastings king of England. He lost no time in bringing Essex
and many other parts of southern England firmly under
Norman control. The result, as far as this county is concerned,
was, as J. Horace Round put it: "There is no county perhaps
that bears more clearly than Essex the imprint of the Norman
Conquest."

Norman nobles established themselves on land granted by
William in return for their support. They made good use of
lesser mortals whose services were available to them under the
terms of the feudal system. They threw up motte and bailey
castles quickly and cheaply. This type of stronghold consisted
of a wooden tower on top of a large earthen mound. Defended
by ditches and ramparts, it provided protection and enabled
the nobleman to dominate the area. Among remains, often
only mounds, are those at Great Canfield (the powerful de
Veres), Pleshey (the de Mandevilles, another powerful family),
and Rayleigh (Sweyn of Essex whose father built the pre-
Norman castle at Clavering).

William himself, determined to exercise strong military
control of England, built royal castles in strategic positions.
One such control point was Colchester castle, a vast structure
built mainly of Roman bricks and dressed stone from the ruins
of the Roman town. Begun about 1085, the castle was a royal
fortress throughout the Middle Ages. Today, though considerably reduced, it is still an impressive building and one that
Colchester in its great wisdom puts to excellent use as the
headquarters of the Colchester and Essex Museum. William's
control was to be based on accurate details of the resources,
human and otherwise, of his kingdom, and so at Christmas
1085 he began the thorough survey whose results appear in
Domesday Book. With only two towns, Colchester and
Maldon, Essex was mainly a county of small villages and
hamlets (438 were named), heavily wooded except along
coast and estuaries, where marshland sheep were common, and
in the north-west. Water mills, fisheries and coastal salt pans
were important economic features and there were vineyards,
too.

The Conqueror died in 1087, but his Norman successors
firmly held to their lands and privileges. In the first half of the
twelfth century the de Veres built their great stone castle,

whose tower-keep is open to visitors at certain times, at Castle Hedingham, near the Suffolk border. About this time, too, the tough and rebellious Geoffrey de Mandeville, first Earl of Essex, built his castle at Saffron Walden. This stronghold was one that worried Henry, Duke of Normandy, when, on becoming king Henry II in 1154, he set about restoring law and order to the kingdom. It had been partially destroyed but the Pipe Rolls, records of royal expenditure, show that in 1158 £9 12s 4d was provided to complete its destruction (only fragments of the flint rubble walling remain).

Certain of the castles mentioned continued for some time to play an exciting part in the history of Essex and England, those at Colchester and Castle Hedingham, for example, being besieged by King John early in the thirteenth century. No less important, though much quieter, was the part played by the churches and monastic houses founded by the Normans, men whose piety might seem inappropriate to their hard and cruel times. About thirty religious houses were founded in Essex during the time of the Norman kings of England and remains of some of them may still be seen. Others have virtually disappeared. Hardly anything survives of the Benedictine priory founded at Earls Colne by Aubrey de Vere, who came over with the Conqueror, but parts of the church of the Benedictine priory founded by his son at Hatfield Broad Oak are embodied in the present church. Remains of the Benedictine priory (later an abbey) founded by Geoffrey de Mandeville at Saffron Walden survive beneath the floors of Audley End. The ravages of men and time, with their heavy toll of monastic buildings, allowed Essex to retain several Norman parish churches. One, the church of St Nicholas at Castle Hedingham, is of particular interest. Built by the de Veres, who lived at the castle, it has marked Norman features as well as some of the Tudor period.

The Normans had ruled throughout the earlier years of the Middle Ages and laid the foundations of the manorial system, one that gave lords of manors considerable powers over the lower orders. But the growth of the woollen industry and other forms of trade and the development of such towns as Chelmsford (the county town by the thirteenth century), Coggeshall, Halstead and Thaxted brought change. The Black

Death of 1348-9 ended the lives of large numbers of the older people in the county, leaving younger people to take over many holdings. Then, in 1381, Essex peasants took an active part in the Peasants' Revolt. The immediate cause of this rising was the imposition of the third poll tax whose collection was openly and sometimes violently resisted in the county. A leading figure in the revolt was John Ball, rector of St James', Colchester, who believed and preached that all men are born equal. Released from prison by the Kentish rebels, he called upon the people to overthrow the government and set up a commonwealth based on social equality and universal brotherhood. England was not ready for this sort of talk and the revolt was ended. John Ball was hanged, drawn and quartered as a traitor in the presence of the king, Richard II, whose promises to the rebels were largely worthless and who was himself murdered nineteen years later.

During the second half of the fifteenth century the county's leading landowners were involved in the Wars of the Roses, the civil wars which resulted in the replacement of the house of Lancaster by the house of York, and eventually in the rise of the house of Tudor. On the Lancastrian side were the Fitzlewes of West Horndon who lost many of their Essex estates during the reign of Edward IV (House of York), and their relatives, the de Veres of Castle Hedingham, two of whom, the twelfth Earl of Oxford and his eldest son, were executed for plotting against the king and preparing for a Lancastrian landing on the east coast. On the Yorkist side were the Bourchiers of Little Easton, Henry, first Earl of Essex of the Bourchier line, being Lord Treasurer to Edward IV who was, in fact, his nephew. When Edward IV's brother Richard III was killed at the battle of Bosworth on 22nd August, 1485, the Wars of the Roses ended. Henry VII began to reign and the Middle Ages ended. Essex was now part of Tudor England.

Both Henry VII and Henry VIII saw to the defence of the realm, fortifying Harwich and raising forts at Landguard Point (actually in Suffolk, but then regarded by Essex as part of her own defences), on Mersea Island and at Tilbury to guard the rivers Orwell-Stour, Colne and Thames respectively. Between them Henry VIII and Parliament substituted the royal supremacy for papal power in England and suppressed the monasteries. This resulted in the loss of much monastic property whose destruction enabled influential people to acquire property and wealth, and whose ruins still bear witness to the time when a king could behead two wives and marry a second wife before the first was divorced. In Colchester St Botolph's Priory and its possessions were granted to Sir Thomas Audley, Lord Chancellor, while St John's Abbey, whose last abbot, John Beche, was hanged in 1539, eventually passed to John Lucas, town clerk and lawyer, whose descendant, Sir Charles Lucas, was one of the Royalist commanders in the Siege of Colchester in 1648. Richard Rich, first Baron Rich of Leighs (or Leez) Priory had rich pickings, acquiring Leighs Priory and many other properties. And so one could continue the sorry tale of worldly men stooping low to line their own pockets.

The Lucas home at St John's Abbey, Colchester, and the Rich family home at Leighs Priory were just two of many Essex houses visited by Elizabeth I during her progresses. During the short reign of her predecessor, Queen Mary, Protestants were persecuted, but during Elizabeth's own reign sanctuary was found in Colchester for Protestant weavers who had fled from the Low Countries, then under Catholic Spanish rule. Colchester was well rewarded, for these honest and industrious folk revitalized the cloth trade, making a significant contribution to the economic life of Essex out of all proportion to their numbers.

On the death of Elizabeth I, James I began to reign and soon friction arose between Crown and Parliament. Charles I succeeded to the throne in 1625. Within a year or two Sir Francis Barrington of Hatfield Broad Oak, whose wife was aunt of the Lord Protector, Oliver Cromwell, stated that he would rather go to prison than lend money to the king under compulsion. He was not the only one who felt this way and, in a county that was strongly parliamentarian, Charles I's attempt to govern without parliament naturally created opposition. The start of the first civil war (1642-6) saw Essex strengthening parliament's forces by joining with other eastern counties in the Eastern Association whose aim was to defend East Anglia. The first civil war ended with the defeat of the royalist cause and the surrender of Charles to the Scots. The second civil war (1648) followed his rejection of proposals submitted by the council of the army and his 'engagement' with the Scots, with its provision for an invasion of England and a royalist rising.

The prospect of military government frightened many people and on 4th May, 1648, the people of Essex presented a petition supported by 30,000 names to Parliament begging for peace with the king. On 4th June a mob at Chelmsford arrested the county committee who were discussing the royalist threat. Four days later two forces fighting for the royalist side, men from Kent under the Earl of Norwich and men from Essex under Sir Charles Lucas, met at Brentwood. After occupying Chelmsford, they moved to Braintree and then made for Colchester where, after some argument, they were admitted. After being besieged by parliamentary forces under General 'Black Tom' Fairfax for eleven weeks, during which there was considerable hostility from starving townspeople and severe damage from the besiegers' fire (signs of this are still visible), the royalist forces surrendered. Sir Charles Lucas, a Colchester man, and Sir George Lisle, another of the chief defenders of the town, were executed. Their fellow officers were held to ransom, the ordinary soldiers sent to the West Indies to work on sugar plantations, and the townspeople heavily fined and ordered to destroy their defences.

During the period between the execution of Charles I and the recall of his son Charles II, trouble between the English and the Dutch developed, resulting in the first Dutch war (1652-4) in which the English navy did well. Harwich played an important part during the second Dutch war (1665-7) when the English fleet used the Gunfleet, a sandbank off the Essex coast opposite Dovercourt, as anchorage. In June 1667 the Dutch, aware that Charles II had virtually disbanded his fleet, entered the Thames, raided Canvey Island and fired broadsides at East Tilbury Church. Later they entered the Medway, but their plan to attack Harwich failed, largely because of the presence of Landguard fort on the Suffolk side of the estuary. The third Dutch war (1672-4) again found the English fleet, this time combined with that of the French, using the anchorage at the Gunfleet. They were there just before moving up the coast to Southwold Bay (Sole Bay) where the battle ended in a draw between the English and the Dutch, the French having taken little part.

Just as the second Dutch war was beginning, bubonic plague had broken out and the Great Plague raged. Colchester, where the siege had brought trade to a standstill, suffered badly and nearly 5,000 people died. Braintree was stricken and Brentwood and other towns near London were seriously affected.

Other sad events disturbed Stuart Essex. Violent action against Roman Catholics resulted from the Popish Plot of 1678, a fictitious conspiracy to murder Charles II and enthrone the Roman Catholic Duke of York with the aid of French and Irish troops. Denounced by Titus Oates, one of the evil authors of the plot, the distinguished Essex royalist William, fourth Lord Petre, died of ill-health in the Tower where he had been imprisoned for five years without trial. The following year, 1685, Charles II died. His brother, James II, succeeded him. During his short reign he undertook to suspend all penal laws against Catholics and Dissenters (Nonconformists), allowing freedom of public worship, and he appointed John, fifth Lord Petre, Lord Lieutenant of Essex.

After the glorious revolution William and Mary reigned and Roman Catholics were penalized. Protestant nonconformists were allowed their own places of worship, teachers and preachers, subject to certain oaths and declarations. The Quarter Sessions papers of the time include records of the licensing of a Quaker meeting house at Thaxted (1695) and a Congregational chapel at Little Baddow (1708).

During the Georgian period Essex was still very largely agricultural, a region of peace and quiet to which Londoners of means escaped and one that provided the capital with meat, fruit, vegetables and other supplies. For some time there was little to disturb the county, though an association was formed at Chelmsford to support George II when, in the Forty-five Rebellion, Prince Charles Edward Stewart, the Young Pretender, attempted a rising.

During the Napoleonic Wars Colchester became a garrison town and martello towers were erected against the threat of French invasion at Clacton, St Osyth and Walton-on-the-Naze. These low round towers were modelled upon a tower at Cap Mortella, Corsica, which offered strong resistance to a British attack in 1794. In 1798 Robert Edward, ninth Lord

Petre, raised and equipped a body of 250 men for the defence of the country. But this tireless worker for Catholic emancipation, whose efforts had borne some fruit a few years earlier, was refused permission for his son, also a Catholic, to take command. The Essex cloth trade ended during the Napoleonic Wars. With the Courtaulds now in this business, however, the silk industry soon began to contribute to the economic life of the county. Now the name Courtauld is known and respected throughout the world, and in this closing quarter of the twentieth century we are able to admire fine Georgian houses in several parts of Essex.

The long reign of Queen Victoria, who came to the throne in 1837, was one of marked change and development in many fields of activity. At first a county of prosperous farming greatly influenced, even dominated in places, by the land-owners, parts of Essex suffered badly during the 'great depression' in agriculture in the 1870s. In some places tenants could not be found for land and certain of the great landed estates already showed signs of breaking up. Nearer the end of the nineteenth century Scotsmen arrived to farm in the county. There was talk of the 'Scotch colony' around Ongar, Brentwood and Chelmsford, and today the descendants of these hard-working and enterprising people form a vital and respected element in the county's agricultural community.

In 1886 the growth of the Port of London involved the building of an extensive system of docks at Tilbury, still included in the county of Essex and now a major centre for freight, container and passenger services to all parts of the world. The railways, too, developed considerably during Queen Victoria's reign. In 1839 the railway between Mile End and Romford, now in Greater London, was opened, and in 1843 the railway from London reached Colchester. Then came lines to Cambridge (passing through west Essex), to Tilbury and Southend, and those that served the Stour and Colne Valleys. This railway network assisted industrial expansion in Colchester and other areas and encouraged the development of resorts such as Southend.

Victorian expansion and development resulted in the erection of countless terraces of dwellings, still such a feature of the older towns and suburbs, and of factories, many of which are still in use. Churches were built and restored (often 'Victorianized') and public buildings erected at the expense of wealthy and public-spirited industrialists. London expanded into Essex at an alarming rate and areas that once formed part of the county have been swallowed into the vast sprawl of Greater London. Enclosures threatened the entire future of Epping Forest, but a twelve-year struggle ended with its preservation as an open space and, on 6th May, 1882, Queen Victoria herself came to High Beech to dedicate 5,559 acres of the forest to the enjoyment of her people 'for ever'.

Victorian Essex, with its great concern for self-improvement, built schools and founded societies for the study and enjoyment of many subjects, including – to mention but two – the Essex Archaeological Society in 1852 and the Essex Field Club in 1880. But, on the darker side, there was the workhouse, central feature of Poor Law relief under the 1834 Act. The inmates derived very little, if any, comfort from the fact that Billericay and Great Dunmow workhouses were designed by the young George Gilbert Scott, who later restored cathedrals, was knighted and finally buried in Westminster Abbey. Some idea of the atmosphere in these places can be gained from a document in the Essex Record Office. This records that the Board of Guardians, having "resolved and ordered" that the inmates of Chelmsford Union Workhouse be allowed the usual Christmas dinner of beef and plum pudding and one pint of beer per head, dealt with a case of inmates accused of bad conduct. Four men, who had "used threats of resisting their separation from their wives", were not to be allowed the usual Christmas dinner and were to attend the Board and be reprimanded. No doubt the Guardians then returned to their cluttered Victorian houses, their castles, leaving the poor men at their gate, all, according to the writer of "All things bright and beautiful", as God had ordered it.

Not all the Victorian poor stood at their gates. Some joined the army, others the navy, serving in many parts of the British Empire. Memorials and trophies of the Essex Regiment in the Regimental chapel and museum at Little Warley serve to remind us of those days. With Queen Victoria's death in 1901, came the end of the Victorian age, the start of the twentieth century, with its own vast changes and startling developments, the decline of the railways, the real beginning of the age of the motor car and aircraft, and, within such a short time, the outbreak of the First World War during which so many people were personally affected by the appalling loss of life and destruction.

Zeppelins passed over the area, one coming down at Little Wigborough in 1916, and when peace was declared in 1918, the submarines and destroyers of the German High Seas Fleet were brought into Harwich to surrender. It is a bitter and sad comment on our times that within twenty-one years German E-boats should again be approaching this Essex port, this time to lay mines, one of which caused the loss of the destroyer HMS *Gypsy* and almost all hands. As in the Great War, many men and women from Essex served in the various theatres of action during the Second World War. Many of them are still experiencing the effects of the political, economic and social changes resulting from that war and its aftermath. They may have their doubts and uncertainties as the years pass, but they may be quite certain that their efforts and sacrifices helped to save Britain from occupation and perhaps virtual destruction. Thanks to them and to those who accepted challenges and hazards that civilians are not normally expected to face, there is still an Essex scene and Englishmen are still free to write about it.

II

THE ESSEX COAST

In parts the Essex coast is not always as easily accessible as many people would like. Certain stretches are, it is true, remote from major roads, but the trouble is largely due to the simple fact that, as the famous Elizabethan topographer William Camden said of the county, "the ocean windeth itselfe into it". Another complaint is that much of the Essex seaboard has lost its natural outline or boundary, but history shows that it has been vitally necessary for centuries to embank this coast, which is sinking and generally marshy and low-lying.

Even so, man-made coastal defences have on occasion proved to be inadequate. As recently as the night of 31st January, 1953, the great tide broke through, caused the deaths of 119 Essex people and thousands of livestock, left over 21,000 people homeless, and wrought great damage to industry over large areas of the county. And there is no doubt that the coast will continue to be affected by changing movements and activities of sea, elements and man.

The people of Harwich, at the extreme north of the Essex coast, realise this only too well. Theirs is not a sheltered life and never has been. We know from the churchwardens' accounts that towards the end of December 1551 two "gret tydes" broke through the west marsh wall at Harwich where men and women worked day and night to repair the damage, sharpening and driving in stakes and bringing in stone, gravel and other kinds of filling. During the following summer a start was made on rebuilding and improving the wall, a task which took three years to complete. Sixteen years later, after a severe storm, the churchwardens paid for repairs to be made to the new work.

Details of much subsequent concern with the sea defences

33

have been lost, but plenty have survived concerning the happenings of 29th November, 1897, when the tide topped the defences and more than 30,000 acres of land were inundated in Essex. No lives were lost on that particular Black Monday, but in Harwich alone 200-300 houses were flooded on Bathside and many people were still imprisoned in them next day. The Bathside wall stood firm during the "highest flood tide within living memory" in January 1928, though some flooding occurred. But the tide broke through it on the night of the 1953 disaster when the sea poured into Harwich from three directions, causing eight people to lose their lives and 1,550 to be made homeless, and resulting in so much damage and contamination that the town was the last place in Essex to return to complete normality.

As for the activities of man, the prosperity of Harwich has waxed and waned over the years. A naval dockyard existed there for many years and naval forces based in the harbour took an active part in the two world wars. Once the home-port of numerous North Sea cod-smacks, Harwich lost two other local industries during the nineteenth century—the manufacture of Roman cement from the local septaria or cement stone and the collection of copperas (bisulphide of iron) from the cliffs. Today, with Britain a member of the EEC, visitors to Harwich view with added interest passenger and cargo ships, container ships and train-ferries, operating to the continent and Scandinavia from the Navyard Wharf, site of the former shipyard, and Parkeston Quay, two miles west up the river Stour. On Harwich Quay Trinity House has its headquarters for Eastern England, the pier where its lighthouse tender ships and pilot cutters berth, and the yard and work-shop where buoys are stored and maintained. Its officers, normally concerned with pilotage, buoys, lightships and light-houses, took an active part in the work of rescue and relief following the 1953 flood disaster.

Old Harwich, now a conservation area watched over by the Harwich Society, readily gives up the history associated with its medieval grid-iron pattern of main streets and narrow connecting alleyways. Near the entrance to the Navyard Wharf is a list of the Men of War constructed in the Old Naval Yard 1660-1827, and the old shipyard bell cast in Ipswich in 1666

and used for more than two hundred years to summon the
workers. What is believed to be the only British example of a
two-wheel man-operated treadwheel crane, a seventeenth-
century relic of the Naval Yard, now stands on Harwich
Green, a stern reminder of harder times. The Redoubt, a
ten-gun fortress standing on top of a hill not far from the
green, formed part of the Martello Tower chain of defences
built to safeguard our coast from the attentions of Napoleon
and his troops.

On the Town Hall, formerly the Great Eastern Railway's
unsuccessful Great Eastern Hotel, a plaque records the town's
connections with the Pilgrim Fathers. The name of the
Mayflower, the ship in which they sailed for America in 1620,
was given in the 1950s to a block of council flats, once a
Salvation Army Red Shield Club for the troops. The
Elizabethan house (rebuilt in the seventeenth century) at 21
Kings Head Street was the home of Christopher Jones who, as
Master and part owner of the *Mayflower*, took the Pilgrims on
their historic voyage to the New World. Both of his marriages
and the baptisms of some of his children are recorded in the
church registers, which date back to 1559. The Alma Inn, an
Elizabethan timber-framed and plastered house with a
Georgian front, was built originally for Peter Pett, a wealthy
shipbuilder, whose great-granddaughter, Sarah Twitt, became
Christopher Jones' first wife in 1593. She died ten years later
and within a few months Jones married Josian, widow of
Richard Grey of Harwich. In 1606 and 1607 Jones was master
of a ship named the *Josian*. In 1609 he was Master and quarter
owner of the *Mayflower*, and in 1610 or 1611 both he and the
last-named ship moved to the Port of London where the
village of Rotherhithe remained his home until his death early
in 1622.

At one time Jones, it has been said, was accused of piracy,
and there has been much talk among certain historians of
plotting and bribery to ensure that the Pilgrims were landed
farther north than the Hudson River, the destination stipu-
lated in the *Mayflower's* charter. Readers may care to ponder
A. J. P. Taylor's view that "all sources are suspect" and to con-
sider accepting what appears to be the majority view, namely
that the landing took place at Cape Cod, to the north, because

Jones had to land where he could. Certainly there are instances in the Pilgrim writings of Jones' kindliness and friendship, and Harwich has good reason to remember him with pride.

Unlike Harwich, Dovercourt, whose beaches and recreational facilities have made it "Harwich's holiday resort suburb", was mentioned in the Domesday Survey. Norman work survives in the nave of All Saints church where there are reminders of the unfortunate British expedition to Walcheren, the low-lying island at the mouth of the Scheldt. Those taking part in 1809 are largely forgotten, even the commanders, Lord Chatham and Sir Richard Strachan, being virtually unknown except to interested students and historians. This epigram of the day, summing up the reasons for the failure of the expedition, lies buried in old books:

> Lord Chatham, with his sword undrawn, stood waiting for Sir Richard Strachan;
> Sir Richard, longing to be at 'em, stood waiting for the Earl of Chatham.

Today visitors to the church pass through the lych-gate presented by Queen Victoria in memory of British soldiers buried in the churchyard, particularly those who died from disease contracted during the Walcheren expedition. In the church a window, given by the Queen's grandson, Kaiser Wilhelm II of Germany, commemorates the Germans who were on the same expedition and are buried in the churchyard.

Sad memories of later relations between Britain and Germany are recalled by another monument in Dovercourt. Erected by his employers, the Great Eastern Railway Company, the memorial to Captain Charles Algernon Fryatt, master of the steamship *Brussels*, records his execution by the Germans at Bruges on the 27th July, 1916. Fryatt, whose ship was steaming home from the Hook of Holland when captured by a torpedo-boat flotilla in June 1916, had steered straight for a German submarine when ordered to stop in March of the previous year. His gallantry is also marked by a memorial on Mount Fryatt in Alberta, Canada.

On the main road from Harwich and Dovercourt to Clacton-on-sea are the villages of Great and Little Oakley, each with its church, that at Great Oakley being beautifully set among trees. Much of the area between the Harwich-Clacton road and the sea from Great Oakley down to the neighbour-hood of Thorpe-le-Soken is occupied by marshy ground, islands and creeks, many of them dangerous to negotiate. The importance of this watery wilderness to naturalists was acknow-ledged by the designation of much of it as Hamford Water Site of Special Scientific Interest by the Nature Conservancy Council. Skipper's Island, a reserve of the Essex Naturalists' Trust, forms part of this site. Like much of Horsey Island, a larger island to the east, the highest parts of Skipper's Island consist of London clay covered by rough pastures, bushes and scrub. Lower land, once enclosed saltings, reverted to saltmarsh following breaches of the sea wall. Much time has been given to creating firebreaks and footpaths through thorn and bramble thickets and to repairing the inner sea wall at Skipper's Island whose 160 acres are the haunt of kestrels, gadwall and other birds and the habitat of many interesting insects and plants.

Hamford Water, known locally as Walton Backwaters, popular site for dinghy sailing, and Walton Creek are separated from the North Sea by the Naze, a promontory stretching northwards from the town of Walton-on-the-Naze. Towards the higher, southern end of the Naze stands a high tower built as a sea-mark for Trinity House Corporation in 1720. Walton-on-the-Naze, with its sandy beaches and shallow water, is a popular family resort. According to Norman Scarfe, author of the Shell guide to Essex, "there is no single building to delight the eye". This statement, strictly a matter of opinion, might well be applied to many places which do not give such marvellous views as those gained from the cliffs of the Naze!

It was during the first half of the nineteenth century that hotels and lodging houses sprang up at Walton, then develop-ing as a watering place, largely due to the initiative and enterprise of the Society of Friends at Colchester. Then, as now, coastal erosion was a serious problem. The pier, the earliest surviving example in the county, was started in 1830 as a short structure of 330 feet and extended in about 1898 to its present length of over 2,600 feet. The anglers seen here represent a large fraternity whose hobby can yield both pleasure and profit along the Essex coast, while the famous Walton lifeboat is, as she lies at her mooring here, a gentle reminder of the unstinted service of Essex lifeboatmen over the years.

Frinton-on-Sea is also a developed area, but one with a much more peaceful atmosphere than many other places on our coast. As a town it has a quiet determination to maintain unspoiled its sandy beach, broad cliff-top greensward, and regular tree-lined avenues of pleasant houses. This has occasion-ally led to Frinton being called snobbish and exclusive, but this is not perhaps surprising in a world where character and stability are not always given their just emphasis and where commonsense is often in short supply. What does genuinely surprise one is that tower-blocks of flats, so out of keeping with everything else there, should ever have been allowed in Frinton.

A walk along the sea wall to the south of the town takes one alongside Frinton golf-course, past Sandy Point and Chevaux de frise Point, and on to the sands and shopping centre of Holland-on-Sea, formerly called Little Holland. Great Holland, lying slightly inland between Frinton and Holland-on-Sea, proudly bears its original name. The church, with its Tudor red-brick tower, stands close to the hall where Charles Hicks farmed from 1829 to 1863. His memoirs, published by the Essex County Council in 1972 (see A. F. J. Brown's *Essex People 1750-1900*), tell, among many other things, of smugg-ling, the alarm created by Napoleon's threatened invasion, the flooding of the marshes by high tides, and, most sadly of all, of the plight of "paupers" who, all too often, were simply farm labourers who, due to the course of events, happened to be out of work. One thing that can be said in favour of the local Establishment of Hicks' time is that it was not entirely without charity. In the early 1830s, backed by Chief Constables, magis-trates, special constables, yeomanry and special commissions, it had suppressed the labourers' disturbances, sentenced some to transportation for life and frightened many others. But at about that time of high unemployment these superior beings, these self-appointed gentlemen, did pay out of the Poor Rates for the passage to Canada of several workers from Great Holland. Perhaps our country's loss was Canada's gain.

During the years immediately preceding the time of which we are speaking this part of the Essex coast was regarded as a most unhealthy place, so much so, in fact, that the men detailed to occupy the Martello towers at Clacton were quartered at Weeley. The Martello towers introduced an alien element to Great Clacton, then a village set among fields and meadows and later to give rise to Clacton-on-Sea. Long since incorporated in the modern resort, Great Clacton retains evidence of its earlier history in the form of the remarkable Norman church of St John the Baptist and a few other buildings such as the red-brick (Georgian) Mansion House.

Proposals for the building of a new resort at Clacton had been made as early as the 1820s by the Society of Friends at Colchester but, unable to purchase the necessary land, it turned its attentions to the village of Walton. A sale plan of 1871 shows, as part of the initial development of Clacton, the position of the pier and main approach. Arranged symmetrically on either side of the seaward end of the main approach are sites for promenades, pleasure grounds and villas. Behind this are open spaces and on one side of the main approach a site for lodging houses, shops, library and bazaar, and on the other a site for hotel, yard, stabling and lodging houses.

The Royal Hotel, its front adorned by an iron verandah on the first floor, was built in 1872. The following year saw the opening of the iron pier. Now one of Europe's largest family fun piers, it is a vital feature of 'show-bizzy' Clacton, the 'liveliest' English resort according to a recent English Tourist Board Holidaymakers' Opinion Survey. Undoubtedly the most important year in the resort's history was 1882 when the Great Eastern Railway reached Clacton and greatly assisted its increase in size and popularity. This satisfactory development of Clacton as a seaside resort was, indeed, one element in the failure of the idea of building a dock on land near the coastguard station, a proposal involving Charles Blaber, a Brighton engineer, and Edwin Gilders, a Clacton surveyor, estate agent, coal merchant and brick and lime manufacturer.

To the west of Clacton and separated from it by a golf course and Martello tower is Jaywick Sands whose development has been variously described as "a bungalow township" and "shackery by the sea". The suffix 'wick' surviving in this and many other Essex marshland place-names recalls the fact that throughout the Middle Ages cheeses were made from ewes' milk in dairies ('wiches' or 'wicks') associated with marshland sheepwalks. Later, as in so many places along the coast, there were times when breaches in the walls allowed the sea to flood the Jaywick marshes, preventing agricultural use for a time. Finally the farming depression of the 1930s caused the sale of Jaywick Farm, the breaking up of the land into small building plots and the building of bungalows, many for summer occupation only, on the marsh behind the sea wall. Many enjoyed the fresh sea air and fine clean sands there before disaster struck during the great tide of 1953. Today, in Jaywick, a tablet on the wall of St Christopher's church perpetuates the memory of: "The people of Jaywick Sands who perished in the floods."

To the west of Jaywick, behind St Osyth beach, caravan sites cater for holiday visitors and towards Colne Point creekside chalets are raised off the ground. A short distance from them is a reserve of the Essex Naturalists' Trust, an area mentioned in chapter nine. Between the shore and the village of St Osyth itself lie Wigboro Wick and Cockett Wick Farms. Associated in earlier times with St Osyth's Priory, whose magnificent gatehouse of flint and stone flushwork attracts countless visitors today, they maintained hundreds of cattle and sheep, providing food and revenue for the wealthy religious house, which it would be more correct to call St Osyth's Abbey. The glory of the parish church of St Peter and St Paul, just across the road from the abbey gatehouse, is its sixteenth-century nave whose carved hammerbeam roof is supported by clustered columns and pointed arches of red brick.

Brightlingsea, at the mouth of the River Colne, was originally Brihtric's Island and today it is still largely surrounded by water. Yachting, boat-building and the holiday industry all help to keep this ancient town alive, and there is abundant evidence of them all. The busy Town Hard is the setting for the headquarters of Brightlingsea Yacht Club whose one-hundreth anniversary was marked by the opening in 1974 of a 300-foot floating jetty. In the church of All Saints, standing away from the little town on a hill overlooking the marshes, there is a frieze of over two hundred memorial tablets to Brightlingsea seamen, many of them lost at sea when very young. The idea for these wall-memorials came from the Rev.

Arthur Pertwee who, as vicar during the late nineteenth century, stood aloft in his church tower in stormy weather and, lantern in hand, guided home the local fishermen to safety. He does not figure in a recent list of Essex worthies, those people who are considered to have attained great success in their lives and to have wielded influence both within the county and in national life as a whole. He, in his quiet way, was nevertheless, like many before and since, the salt of the earth. I wonder what he would have made of the learned Sir Nikolaus Pevsner, who regarded this historic limb of the Cinque Port of Sandwich as "not specially attractive". Surely the very attraction of the place is that virtually everything smacks of the sea and ships.

From the southern tip of the Brightlingsea marshes one may look up Brightlingsea Reach towards the open sea and across the mouth of the River Colne to the eastern side of Mersea Island. This oval shaped island, measuring about five miles by two-and-a-half and lying between the mouths of the Rivers Colne and Blackwater, is connected to the mainland by the Strode or Strood, a causeway that is passable except at times of very high tides. Once on the island itself the main road branches into two, one road leading to West Mersea, a growing residential, seaside and yachting centre, the other to East Mersea, a much smaller village. The northern side of the island has a 'Dutch' landscape produced by wide stretches of marshland and great lengths of sea wall, while the southern shore has flat stretches of sand.

The church of St Edmund King and Martyr, with its big Perpendicular stone tower, preserves something of the history of East Mersea. As evidence of West Mersea's past, the church of St Peter and St Paul has parts belonging to the Early Norman period and others to later times. Only 200 yards away is a wheel tomb similar to those found in other parts of the Roman Empire, and Mersea Mount, a mile and a half from the church, is a Romano-British burial mound where the cremated remains of a grown-up person were deposited.

On Mersea and in other parts of the county, the Romans, who ate vast quantities of shellfish, undoubtedly enjoyed the local oysters. A note of near disaster appeared in the long and colourful history of the Essex fisheries when, during the exceptionally hard winter of 1962-3, millions of oysters were killed as the sea in the creeks froze solid. New stock was introduced to ensure the survival of the oyster fishery, but the price of oysters has risen steeply. Another sign of the times is that councillors attending the famous annual Oyster Feast at Colchester are now apparently asked to pay for their tickets. The effect of this change of policy on the future of such a traditional event will be awaited with interest. Certainly the free provision of hospitality in the past did not always leave departing guests in a satisfied frame of mind. The late Lord Brabazon of Tara, who proposed the toast "The art of living" at the 1960 Feast, thought that the lunch was anything but a feast. On the other hand, the late Sir Compton Mackenzie, who responded to that particular toast, thoroughly enjoyed himself. But, then, he had managed to secure thirty Colchester 'Pyefleet' native oysters instead of the six everybody else got! One would have liked to have heard the comments of the "rose-growing, oyster-eating boiler-makers" of whom Colchester used to boast.

From the richly decorated Moot Hall, scene of the Oyster Feast, we return to the coast. Crossing the estuary of the River Blackwater, we reach the flat exposed marshes of the Dengie peninsula which stretch into the distance as far as the estuary of the River Crouch. This is a region where past and present meet in a manner which is both dramatic and uncompromising. At its north tip, at Bradwell-juxta-Mare, the great nuclear power station, begun in 1957, dominates Bradwell Waterside, representing an age of technological materialism. About two miles away the church of St Peter-on-the-wall stands where, in all probability, it has stood since about the year 654. Exposed to the bitter east winds of the North Sea in almost complete isolation, this chapel (as it is now known) was used as a lighthouse in Tudor times and later as a barn before being restored and re-consecrated about 1920. This was one of two centres (Tilbury was the other) from which St Cedd, a Christian teacher, went forth to preach and baptize at the request of Sigebert the Good, King of the pagan East Saxons, who had been baptized by the Bishop of Lindisfarne in 653. The chapel stands on the landward wall of one of the Roman 'Forts of the Saxon Shore', probably that named Othona. Part of a system of defences built to guard the coast against attacks by raiders from across the North Sea, the fort was partially destroyed by the sea, an ancient antagonist along this coast.

Evidence of man's long battle to protect the marshes from inundation by the sea survives here in the form of old sea-walls and farm tracks and roads following the lines of other old walls. Red hills, mounds whose name refers to the colour of their fire-reddened soil, occur in parts of this otherwise flat landscape. These sites of Romano-British saltings, where salt was extracted by heating brine in clay containers, are often of great archaeological interest because of their accumulation of charcoal, broken pots and other objects.

In the past human activity on these coastal marshes of the Dengie peninsular also included the operations of duck-decoy ponds. Marshhouse Decoy Pond, seaward of Tillingham village, was a particularly well-known feature of the marshes. Annual catches of between 700 and 3,000 duck were once made there. The 'wick' place-names—Weatherwick, Bridgewick, Middle Wick, and others—mark the sites of early dairy farms where ewe-milk cheese, or 'whitemeat', and other milk products were made. "In these parts", wrote Norden in the sixteenth century, "are the great and huge cheeses made wondered at for their massiveness and thickness".

South of the Dengie peninsula and the estuary of the River Crouch lies Foulness Island, the largest of a group of low, flat islands whose members are separated from the mainland and from each other by creeks, reaches and other narrow waterways. Most of the small resident population work in farming, producing mainly cereal crops, beef and mutton, or for the Ministry of Defence. Military activities and the ban on general public access have lent the island an atmosphere of mystery. All this began as long ago as the Napoleonic wars when General Shrapnel's new explosive shell was tested there. Now it can be claimed, apparently with complete justification, that the presence of the Ministry of Defence over the years has protected Foulness, enabling it to retain qualities of peace and beauty now far from common in many parts of England.

In earlier times access from the mainland to the island was by ferry or at low water along the Broomway. An ancient trackway marked by hundreds of bunches of poles and twigs, the Broomway crosses the Maplin Sands at a distance of about a quarter of a mile from the shore, covering the six miles from

Wakering Stairs on the mainland to Fisherman's Head on Foulness. This old route, over which the tides move swiftly, has the reputation of being dangerous and certainly many unfortunate people have been trapped and drowned there. However, great use was made of it by those rescuing livestock after the 1953 flood disaster, the Great Tide. Making an experimental journey along the Broomway, one cattle truck successfully evacuated sixteen horses, fourteen calves, fifteen sheep, thirty poultry, a hundred ducks and three pigs. Next day a fleet of twenty-four cattle lorries followed the same route and evacuated most of the cattle.

Like Foulness, the other five islands of the 'Essex Archipelago'—New England, Havengore, Potton, Rushley and Wallasea—were under water following the Great Tide. Like Foulness, too, they were scenes of gallant rescues and evacuations, of colossal efforts to mend and strengthen sea walls whose value is all too often overlooked when tides run normally. Today these lonely farming outposts attract little attention.

Parts of the coast south of Havengore Island also suffered at the time of the Great Tide when valuable assistance rendered to the civil authorities included that of the garrison at Shoeburyness. The military have long occupied this southern promontory. They purchased ground there and set up ranges for the use and practice of artillery about the middle of last century. Trials were held in 1862, after improvements had been made in the construction of cannon to counterbalance the strength given to warships by iron plates, and then, in 1865, the National Artillery Association held its first annual meeting for prize-shooting. The barracks at Shoeburyness occupy the site of an encampment attributed to the Danish chieftain Haestern (circa 894), the "lusty and terrifying old warrior" who had been defeated at the battle of Benfleet. Very few fragments of the ancient camp remain.

The seven mile stretch of coast from Shoeburyness to Leigh-on-Sea is densely built over, well populated, and provided with its own modern airport. But, as an old-established seaside playground, Southend-on-Sea, as the whole area is collectively known, caters not only for those to whom the cheerfully brash acts as a tonic but for others whose pleasure is found in carefully tended parks and gardens, on the golf course, on yachts, and in many other ways.

As a resort, Southend, like so many large and successful enterprises, began in a small way. Sea bathing was becoming fashionable during the second half of the eighteenth century when a few houses and an hotel were built at the south end of Prittlewell, a tiny hamlet called 'Sowthende' in a will of 1481. Visitors arrived but in small numbers. Then, in 1791, a company, which failed within a few years, was formed to develop 'New Southend' as a seaside resort. The Royal Terrace, its houses with balconies or verandahs of cast iron, still stands, a survivor of those early years of the nineteenth century when the delicate Princess Charlotte, only child of George, Prince of Wales (afterwards George IV), stayed there with her mother. Their visits conferred on Southend the patronage that established it as a fashionable holiday resort.

Now regarded as one of the town's star features, Southend pier is noted for its lively entertainment, electric trains and sea fishing. Dating from about 1890, its length of $1\frac{1}{4}$ miles is said to make it unique, a fact which did not discourage the lifeboat crews as they tramped in the early hours to the lifeboat station at the pierhead. There have, in fact, been a number of occasions when prompt action by the lifeboatmen saved Southend pier from being cut in two by drifting craft that were crashing into it. The modern pier's predecessor, a wooden structure of equal length, had been completed in 1846. But five years later the population of Southend was still only 1,141, a small fraction of the figures for two of its competitors, Brighton and Margate. The opening in 1856 of the London, Tilbury and Southend Railway terminus and in 1889 of the direct line through Shenfield stimulated development, and soon day-trippers, mainly from London, outnumbered the wealthy.

Since the Second World War Southend has expanded as a commercial and industrial town, modern office blocks and industrial estates having made their appearance. Southend-on-Sea Municipal Airport has contributed greatly to the development not only of the town but of the surrounding area as a whole. Scheduled and charter air services for passengers, cars and freight operate through this 'gateway to the continent' at Rochford, a wartime satellite base for Hornchurch, headquarters of Number 11 Group, Fighter Command, whose responsibility was the aerial defence of London. Memories of even earlier days are revived by a visit to the Historic Aircraft Museum next to the airport in Aviation Way where Tigers, Gipsys, and Puss Moths are just a few of more than thirty aircraft displayed in "the world's biggest moth collection".

Although Southend has developed in a striking way, it has preserved a number of its old buildings and historical associations. Set in Priory Park, with its old world garden, floral walks and lakes, Prittlewell Priory now houses the South-east Essex Museum of Antiquities and Bygones. Founded about 1110 as a cell of the great Cluniac Benedictine priory at Lewes in Sussex, the original small building was added to several times. Also in a lovely garden setting, Southchurch Hall Museum, a timbered fourteenth-century manor house, retains its central hall open to the roof. There are many old churches, too. The church of St Laurence and All Saints at Eastwood, whose two surviving thirteenth-century doors are of great interest, has Norman features, including a circular font with intersected arches. Norman walls and other Norman evidence such as two small blocked windows form part of the large church of the Annunciation of the Blessed Virgin Mary at Prittlewell. The small Norman church at Southchurch became an aisle of Holy Trinity, a larger church built in 1906, while St Andrew's at South Shoebury, though added to throughout the centuries, has a Norman nave and chancel.

At Hadleigh, close to Southend, the little church of St James the Less is Norman with very few later additions. Away from its rather noisy surroundings a minor road leads to the ruins of Hadleigh castle. Built originally early in the thirteenth century, it became familiar to many who had never visited the site as the subject of John Constable's great painting, the full-scale study for which is in the Tate Gallery, London. Much less familiar are the remarkable life and work of the original builder of Hadleigh castle, Hubert de Burgh, Chief Justiciar of England, who died in 1243, twelve years after completing the building.

Of Norman-Irish birth, he was employed by Richard I. Later he acted as envoy from King John on a number of occasions, was chamberlain to the king and may have been gaoler of John's nephew Arthur, who was in the eyes of many people Richard's rightful heir. De Burgh figures in Shakespeare's *King John* on the strength of a story derived from the chronicle of Ralph de Coggeshall, abbot of Coggeshall, Essex. In 1215, the year he was appointed justiciar, he became a conservator of Magna Carta. He continued to hold office when the young Henry III succeeded his father John in 1216. Between 1219, when the regent died, and 1227, the year Henry assumed royal power, de Burgh was a powerful figure in the land, adding to such earlier achievements as the defence of Dover Castle against the French, and the destruction of the French fleet off the North Foreland, the defeat of the nobles' plot to seize the king. In 1229 he was violently attacked by this same king, because of lack of money in the treasury, and two years later, just as the building of Hadleigh Castle was completed, his enemies saw to it that he lost power, property and offices. Accused of many crimes and imprisoned, he escaped and was outlawed, and it was not until 1234 that his outlawry was reversed and another five years passed before he was acquitted of the charges levelled against him.

From the spur of high ground where Edward III rebuilt Hadleigh Castle one overlooks low-lying pastures and the Thames estuary in an area where planning permission has been granted for the establishment of the 1,584-acre Hadleigh Castle Country Park. This is to contain a sizeable nature reserve, but before any move was made to bring the land into public ownership extensive scrub clearance took place and a badger sett was bulldozed.

This is not the first time that idealistic plans have been made for the use of land in this area. Hadleigh Castle was included in some 1,000 acres bought by General Booth in 1891 for the establishment of the Salvation Army's first Farm Colony. The purpose of this type of colony was to teach skills to destitute recruits from city slums, representatives of "the submerged tenth" which the General wanted to eliminate. The Salvation Army publication *Hadleigh: The Story of a Great Endeavour* describes the object of the colony as being:

. . . to give employment (and food and lodging in return for his labour) to any able-bodied man who is willing to work. It provides food, work, and shelter for destitute able-bodied men of all classes (the titled scapegraces who have sojourned on the colony are not few), creeds, nationalities, and colours, fits them by discipline, care, and kindness to take their places again in society; sends them when reformed back to their friends, to situations, to other lands, or permits them to settle and shelter permanently under its own Flag.'

Nine superintendents watched over the colony's activities, some idea of which can be gained from advertisements issued late last century. One announced that, with an output of 250,000 per week, the colony was in a position to supply the local and the London market with good saleable bricks at moderate prices. Another offered to supply poultry and eggs for hatching from the poultry farm whose reputation had resulted in "world-wide celebrity". Others concerned the sale of Hadleigh Middle White Yorkshire pigs and of cut blooms, pot plants, seedlings, tomatoes and cucumbers from the nurseries.

This was not simply sales talk, for the colony was successful in both material and human terms. In one year alone, during the 1920s, about a thousand young men went out to the Dominions after completing their training there. Although the colony no longer operates according to the original plan, the Salvation Army retains a foothold at Hadleigh and is, of course, active not only in many other parts of Essex but also in widely separated places throughout the world. No man can ever hope to even estimate the extent of the colony's influence. But of one thing we may be certain: any person or organisation whose activities uplift the spirit of a single individual is by any definition a force for good and one to be respected.

Between Hadleigh Castle and the Thames, and separated from the Essex mainland by the narrow Benfleet Creek, lies Canvey Island whose walling-in, drainage and reclamation from the sea took place in the seventeenth century. Joas Croppenburgh, a Dutch citizen and haberdasher of London, undertook to do the work at his own expense in return for one third of the land reclaimed. Croppenburgh married the great-niece of Sir Cornelius Vermuyden, the Dutch engineer who drained the Fens. He employed Dutchmen and many of them settled on the island where two of their octagonal thatched cottages, dated 1621 and 1618, survive.

Arable farming at Wix

Wheatfields near Bradfield

Billericay: the Chequers Inn

Town Hall, Harlow New Town

Basildon

West Stockwell Street, Colchester

Chelmsford: the Cathedral

The River Chelmer, near Little Baddow

Certain 'newlands' were reclaimed during the nineteenth century, but by 1851, the year of the Great Exhibition, the population of the island was only 111. Then, in 1901, Frederick Hester acquired land there and divided it into small building plots. He enabled people to buy these on the instalment system, and the island's population began to increase. One hundred years after Prince Albert's Great Exhibition the figure had risen to 11,258, and Canvey Island had become not only a residential area but an industrial centre and a holiday resort with beaches, amusement centres and shops.

During the period 1851–1951 the sea wall – the structure considered to be practically invulnerable by Hester's supporters – withstood a number of batterings. But 1953 found it unequal to the exceptional fury of the Great Tide and floodwater poured over much of the island, causing the loss of fifty-eight lives and considerable damage, and enforcing the evacuation of a large part of the population. Eventually, with people returning to their homes, it was decided to build sea defences three feet above the 1953 level to protect the island's eastern residential area and two feet above it in the agricultural area.

On Canvey Island during the first year of restoration and reinforcement of the defences, 1953–4, over half a million cubic yards of clay were dug and deposited on the sea wall, 2,000 tons of interlocking steel sheet piles were driven along a 5½ mile frontage, five miles of secondhand tramrail were used to reinforce the piling, and 350,000 concrete blocks were added to the outer face of the sea wall.

Today the island's sea wall is a reminder of the Great Tide and of the enormous powers of wind and water. The 'King Canute' is another. On one side of its sign King Canute admonishes the heedless waves, while on the other men toil to mend the island's wall. Inside, in the saloon bar, an oak plaque explains that this hostelry, then known as the 'Red Cow', was used as headquarters by those engaged in the epic defence and rebuilding of the sea wall breached by floods during the Great Tide. "At this very point", the visitor is informed, "the waters ebbed and hence it was renamed the 'King Canute'."

From the sea wall on the southern side of Canvey Island one may look across the Thames towards Kent. Standing there one recalls that many links exist between the two counties of Essex and Kent. An historic one was forged in 1442 when Bright-lingsea was made a limb of Sandwich, one of the Cinque Ports whose jurisdiction was vested in barons, called wardens, for the better security of the coast.

More recent, but nonetheless interesting, connections between the two counties occurred in the nineteenth century when the Commissioners of Sewers appealed to Kent for supplies of Kentish Ragstone for use in their work of repairing and strengthening the walls of Canvey Island. It was from Kent, too, that these same Commissioners obtained the help in 1864 of a Mr Elliot, a leading drainage engineer from the Romney Marsh district, who surveyed the Canvey Island wall between Holehaven and Thorney Creek. His advice does not appear to have been followed and in 1881 part of this southern wall collapsed and 1,200 acres were inundated and £10,000-worth of damage done.

Looking towards the Kentish marshes of Halstow and St Mary's from this southern side of Canvey, one also recalls that in 1953, at the time of the Great Tide, Kent, like Essex, suffered severe flooding, more than seventy eight square miles of its low-lying ground being inundated. Also like Essex, it has recovered from the disaster, but both counties know only too well that where the sea is concerned eternal vigilance is essential.

III

THE RIVERS

"No one can claim to know the county until he has followed the rivers to their source." Harold Shelton wrote those words many years ago and they still contain much truth. Not everyone has the time or inclination to be guided by them, but most of us must surely appreciate not only the importance of rivers as drainage channels and sources of water but as vital features in landscape and in commercial and leisure interests.

Running along the northern boundary of the county, uniting, rather than dividing, Essex and Suffolk, the River Stour rises in the north-west corner of its catchment, near Weston Green in Cambridgeshire. Undoubtedly the most loved part of its valley is Dedham Vale, the area of outstanding natural beauty dubbed 'Constable's country'. Dedham itself is the lovely village where John Constable attended the Grammar School, walking there each day through the shaded lane depicted in the *Cornfield* (National Gallery, London). Constable felt a deep love for this small area of English countryside. "I associate my 'careless boyhood'", he wrote in 1821, "with all that lies on the banks of the Stour. Those scenes made me a painter, and I am grateful – that is, I had often thought of pictures before I ever touched a pencil."

Today Dedham, on the Essex side of the Stour, copes magnificently with the large numbers of visitors who come to see its fine parish church of St Mary and its Georgian-fronted houses. There is an old-world charm and distinction about the place, its well-stocked shops included, and one feels an immense sense of gratitude towards the Dedham Vale Society, which exists to maintain, protect and enhance the natural, architectural and other amenities of the vale. The Society is interested in the preservation of the River Stour as a quiet waterway for rowing-boats and canoes, and for the enjoyment of anglers.

Another body, the River Stour Trust, seeks cooperation with everyone concerned with the river to ensure that it is not monopolised by any one particular interest. The River Stour was made navigable by Act of Parliament in 1705 and the public right to pass along it from Sudbury to the sea remains. Set up in 1968 to protect and enhance this public right to navigate, the trust has already re-opened Flatford Lock and built several landing stages to enable small craft to negotiate the many obstructions in the river.

The River Stour was once noted for its numerous water-mills and, though they are not in working order, it is still controlled by sluice gates or weirs at the sites of many of them. Nowadays the river, whose waters are carefully guarded against pollution, is an important source of water for South Essex, up to forty seven million gallons per day being ab-stracted at Langham and Stratford St Mary and pumped into Abberton Reservoir near Colchester, which also receives water taken from the Stour at Brantham. This last-named place is close to the head of the estuary into which the Stour passes before joing the waters of the River Orwell and flowing into the North Sea through Harwich Harbour.

Flowing into the same stretch of ocean further down the Essex coast is the River Colne. Rising near the Suffolk border, about 1½ miles south of the village of Steeple Bumpstead, whose church tower and chancel are of eleventh-century origin, it almost dries up in summer in the early part of its course. Flowing generally eastwards to Great Yeldham, where the fifteenth-century timbered 'White Hart' stands in neat road-side grounds, the Colne turns southeastwards through Sible Hedingham. This large industrialized village, birthplace of Sir John Hawkwood, celebrated fourteenth-century de-fender of the liberties of Florence, is not as well-known as neighbouring Castle Hedingham where the de Veres, Earls of Oxford and one of the most powerful families of Norman England, built the dominating castle whose tower-keep is well preserved.

Moving towards the sea, the Colne reaches Halstead where Courtauld's Mill forms an artificial obstruction to its flow (there are many more along its course). Halstead, pleasant main town of the Colne Valley, has a market and many industries, several old buildings and extensive new housing estates. Flowing eastwards, the river reaches Earls Colne, its church tower decorated with the arms of the de Veres who were buried in the Benedictine priory church, and then goes on to Wakes Colne, a small village looking across to Chappel, with its thirty-arch brick railway viaduct.

Winding across country, twisting and turning, the River Colne eventually reaches, at a point about thirty-two miles from its source, the tidal limit at East Mills, Colchester. The tidal river flows south from here, through the Hythe, the port of Colchester, whose trade has increased since the Second World War, to join the sea between St Osyth Point and Mersea Point. On its journey it passes Wivenhoe, once important as a port for fishing boats but now mainly known for ship-building. The old buildings on the quay, and the magnificent example of pargetting (relief plasterwork) on the Garrison House, make this little town, the birthplace of the dandy Beau Brummell, well worth visiting.

Further along the Colne, on the Alresford side, are two sites of Roman villas, while on the other bank at Fingringhoe is the site of what was probably a Roman military supply depot. In this region of creeks and channels, lonely saltings and islands, it is not difficult to imagine oneself transported back to earlier times when these sites were alive, their occupants busy receiving troops and supplies from the continent.

Similarly one could easily conjure up visions of tenth-century activity just down the coast, in the estuary of the River Blackwater, site of Northey Island, encampment of Viking invaders who beat Britnoth's defence-force in the epic Battle of Maldon (991). Known in its upper reaches above Bocking as the Pant, the River Blackwater rises a few miles south-east of Saffron Walden. Flowing almost due south-east, it passes through twenty-six parishes before reaching its tidal limit. Close to the source are Wimbish, its church with a Norman nave, and Radwinter with much work of the nineteenth-century architect Eden Nesfield. Great and Little Sampford are next on the Pant's journey towards the sea. They have interesting churches, but the first-named village is particularly lovely, though the latter has a fifteenth-century, moated manor house. Then come Great and Little Bardfield. Each is attractive in its own way, but Great Bardfield has its Cottage Museum, "the corn dolly centre", where corn-dolly making courses are held in autumn.

On through the farming country of northern Essex the Pant reaches Wethersfield whose triangular green is the centre of a village whose visual qualities are often thought to be as effective as those of the nearby but much more popular Finchingfield. By the river at Shalford stands the medieval church, its altar decorated with strawplaiting from the 1872 exhibition. Passing holdings with such names as Rotten End Farm, Iron Bridge Farm, Goldsticks Farm, and Little Priory Farm, the Pant arrives at Bocking. Now linked, Braintree and Bocking form a manufacturing town whose ties with the U.S.A. originated in 1632 when the 'Braintree Company' sailed for New England, there to found the town of Braintree in what is now the State of Massachusetts.

From this point the river, now known as the Blackwater, passes on to Stisted, its rectory described in the pages of E. M. Forster's biography of his great-aunt, Marianne Thornton, and then to Bradwell whose church has fourteenth-century wall paintings and a monument to William Maxey, Justice of the Peace, who got his children up by 5 a.m. "and caused them to demand his blessing upon their knees". From Coggeshall, a conservation area with the richly ornamented Paycockes and other fine houses, the Blackwater flows south-west to the picturesque village of Feering and then on to Kelvedon, birth-place of C. H. Spurgeon, the famous preacher. Further on, south of Little Braxted, the river is joined by its largest tributary, the Brain, which is known from its source just south of Great Bardfield to immediately upstream of Braintree as Pods Brook.

Now flowing through wooded country, the Blackwater arrives at Wickham Bishops, a large village with two churches, one ancient and being lovingly restored by the Friends of Friendless Churches, the other Victorian. Finally the Black-water reaches its tidal limit at Langford. Here water is ab-stracted from both it and the River Chelmer (about which more will be said later), some being treated for use in Southend, the rest being pumped to Hanningfield Reservoir, south-west of Maldon, to be treated and distributed to

Southend, Basildon and south-west Essex.

Beyond Langford the Blackwater becomes part of the Chelmer and Blackwater Navigation, the canal opened in 1797, whose commercial life of nearly 180 years has ended, resulting in it being given over to amenity use by the public. Eventually the navigation continues through a long artificial cut to Heybridge Basin, which accommodated sea-going coal and timber ships of 300 tons, leaving the rivers Blackwater and Chelmer to discharge into the tidal river flowing to Maldon at the head of the Blackwater Estuary.

Maldon, an ancient Charter Borough, climbs its bold hill from the waters of the two rivers. The High Street, the centre of the town, has many old buildings, some hidden behind modern shop fronts. At the top of this street is All Saints' Church whose unique triangular west tower dates from the thirteenth century. One of this building's many interesting features is the memorial window to Laurence Washington, great-great-grandfather of the first American President, who was rector of nearby Purleigh from 1632 until 1643. Opposite the church is the 'King's Head', an inn for over 400 years, and also in the town centre is the 'Blue Boar', the property of the de Veres, Earls of Oxford, before it became an inn in 1573. Like the 'Blue Boar', the Moot Hall gives a false impression of its age to the casual onlooker: it was, in fact, built in the second half of the fifteenth century as a corner tower of the d'Arcy family's uncompleted mansion.

The visitor who, leaving High Street, makes for the Hythe will find even further evidence of Maldon's long history for here, close to the riverside, stands the church of St Mary the Virgin whose tower was once an important beaconed sea mark. Seen in sunlight from the Marine Parade, a delightful waterside promenade, or from the far side of the Marine Lake, St Mary's is a splendid sight. Set among trees and appearing to be guarded by masts of barges at the quay, it leaves one with a pleasant memory of a friendly and welcoming little town.

Intimate partner of the Blackwater near the end of its run to the sea, the River Chelmer rises in the north of the county, in Rowney Wood, one mile east of Debden, an attractive village set in a region of scattered farmhouses. Commencing in an easterly direction, the young river, its course not straight for

long, then flows towards the south, passing to the west of
Thaxted whose great church attracts thousands of visitors each
year to the quiet little town. Flowing through countryside once
loved by monks of the Cistercian Abbey at Tilty (their
'chapel-outside-the-gate' survives as the parish church), and
watched over by the occupants of the motte-and-bailey castle
at Great Easton, the Chelmer reaches Great Dunmow where
the famous annual Flitch Trial is now held, and Little
Dunmow, scene of the origin of this custom of awarding a
flitch of bacon to a married couple who "have not offended
their marriage for a year and a day."

At Felsted the Chelmer is joined by one of its principal
tributaries, the Stebbing Brook from Lindsell whose small
church of pebble rubble with red-brick dressings has been
described as one of the most delightful in England. Felsted itself
is noted for the boys' public school founded in the sixteenth
century and the brewery by the river at Hartford End has long
been celebrated for its excellent real ale.

Great Waltham stretches along the Chelmer's west bank
from Felsted almost to Chelmsford. A pleasant village, it has
two old inns – the 'Six Bells' on the south side of the
churchyard and, at Howe Street, the fourteenth-century
'Green Man'. Langleys, a large brick mansion incorporating
some of the original early seventeenth-century house, stands in
lovely grounds that run down to the river. Across the river
from Great Waltham is Little Waltham, another pleasant
village, its church partly Norman.

Flowing on to Broomfield, the Chelmer next passes through
Springfield and then into the built-up area of the county town
itself. Passing under railway and roads, it is joined in
Chelmsford by its tributary the River Can from the Easters –
High Easter and Good Easter. Partly Norman, with Roman
bricks in quoins and walling, the church at High Easter is close
to fifteenth-century timber-framed and gabled houses. That at
Good Easter has thirteenth-century nave and chancel.

On the western side of Chelmsford the River Can has been
joined by its major tributary, the Wid. This river rises in the
area north of Blackmore whose Norman church, with its
impressive fifteenth-century timber tower, is an attractive
feature of this developing village to the east of Chipping Ongar.

Flowing southwards the Wid passes to the south of Mount-nessing where Essex County Council owns the post mill, whose brick roundhouse is uniquely sixteen-sided, and where the seven-bay brick Mountnessing Hall makes a handsome group with the church of St Giles. Turning to the north-east, the river passes to the east of Ingatestone. Here Ingatestone Hall, a many-gabled house, was built round a courtyard for Sir William Petre, who became Principal Secretary to Henry VIII and survived to hold office under Edward, Mary and Elizabeth. The house is still owned by the Petre family, part of it being leased to Essex County Council as a centre for annual exhibitions of historical records. Among the portraits in the Long Gallery is one of Robert Edward, ninth Lord Petre (1742-1801), active supporter of the movement for Catholic Emancipation which led to the Catholic Relief Acts (1782, 1791) and the Catholic Emancipation Act (1829). His memory should surely be cherished by all who value tolerance.

At Margaretting, by which the Wid now flows, St Margaret's has a splendid fifteenth-century timber tower on ten posts (as at Blackmore, already mentioned). This church contains a Tudor brass showing Robert Sedge and his wife who lived at Killigrews, a moated Tudor house that survives with later additions. Threading its way beneath roads and railway, the Wid passes through Widford and then Writtle, with its attractive village green, to its confluence with the Can.

On the eastern side of Chelmsford, the River Chelmer, having been joined here by the Can, becomes part of the Chelmer and Blackwater Navigation Canal and passes through some beautiful countryside, much of which can be viewed by the public in the comfort of the Canal Company's pleasure cruiser *Victoria*. With its head in Chelmsford, in Springfield Basin, the navigation joins the River Chelmer just below Springfield Lock. Near Barnes Mill Lock the canal passes a late eighteenth-century mill, later taking an artificial cut to bypass the site of Sandford Mill where formerly much waterborne wheat was ground and where just over fifty years ago Chelmsford Council established its waterworks to treat water drawn from the navigation.

Later, between Cuton Lock and Stoneham's Lock, there is a good view of Danbury Hill, a landmark with its spired church.

At Little Baddow Lock a house stands on the site of a mill that was destroyed late last century. From the navigation beyond Boreham Bridge one sees Little Baddow church standing opposite the Hall, a beautiful fourteenth-fifteenth century timber-framed house. At Paper Mill Lock, Little Baddow, half way mark along the navigation in barging days, are stables used for the horses that drew the barges and a bothy (recently restored) where the bargees spent the night. This lock owes its name to the paper mill that once stood on the 'island' nearby (corn was ground in another mill here).

Next is Rushes Lock, immediately below which the River Ter, a tributary of the River Chelmer, discharges into the navigation. From its source at Yewtree Farm, one mile east of Stebbing church (itself notable for the great fourteenth-century stone rood screen that fills the tall chancel arch) the River Ter flows initially in a general south-easterly direction to Stebbing Green, site of a Roman building, Frenches Green, and Molehill Green where it turns sharply towards Thistley Green. Here it turns sharply again, this time eastwards for $1\frac{1}{4}$ miles, passing the remains of Leighs (or Leez) Priory where, in the sixteenth century, Lord Rich pulled down most of the monastic buildings and built himself an ornamented red brick mansion, much of which was razed during the eighteenth century. Just east of the priory, reservoirs of 100 million gallon capacity are filled by pumping from the river in winter, water being released in summer to compensate for abstractions downstream to fill smaller irrigation reservoirs.

Turning here to the south-east, the Ter flows through Little Leighs, its church containing a beautiful early fourteenth-century carved oak figure of a priest in cope, scarf and alb, passes Sandy Wood and then continues through the attractive village of Terling. Leaving farmland and parkland, the river goes under railway and road at Hatfield Peverel, a large and growing village and the largest centre of population in its catchment area of thirty two square miles. Finally the Ter meanders away from noise and bustle for the last $2\frac{1}{2}$ miles of its course to the Chelmer, here, as we have seen, part of the Chelmer and Blackwater Navigation Canal.

Beyond Rushes Lock and the point of entry of the Ter is Ulting church. Set by the river, All Saints is mainly thirteenth century. Next along the navigation, in an artificial cut which bypassed the mill that stood here until about 1914, is Hoe Mill Lock, and a short distance below this is Sugar Baker's Holes, site of one of the earliest beet sugar works in Britain. Rickett's Lock, with one of the original red brick bridges built on the navigation late in the eighteenth century, is next, and then there is Beeleigh Lock in the artificial cut joining the Rivers Chelmer and Blackwater near the end of their journeys to the sea. Beeleigh Abbey is pleasantly situated here, by the river, a picturesque reminder of the much larger abbey founded about 1180 for Premonstratensian canons.

The Blackwater runs out to sea along the northern edge of the Dengie peninsular, the River Crouch doing so along its southern side. The Battle River, as the Crouch has been called, rises in the area of Friern Manor south of Billericay, flowing eastwards past Crays Hall Farm, between Ramsden Bellhouse and Ramsden Crays (now known as Crays Hill), and on to Wickford. As recently as 1901 the population of Wickford, now a modern residential town, was only 638. Within fifty years it had increased to 8,000 and at April 1974 was estimated to be 24,000. The town has its own industrial estate of about twenty-three acres where various types of light industry are carried on, and it is proud of its amenities, including a modern swimming-pool and, in the fifty-six-acre Wickford Memorial Park, Table House, a building provided by Wickford Round Table as a holiday home for educationally sub-normal children.

Flowing on, the River Crouch reaches Battlesbridge, much of which is included in Rettendon whose church of All Saints contains a large marble monument to Edmund Humphrey who died a bachelor, leaving his estates to friends. Beyond Fenn Creek, on the northern side of the river is South Woodham Ferrers. Essex County Council plan to create here a small country town with a balanced community and full services for a high quality of life for residents, developing the existing village area with a population of 4,000 into a centre whose population will eventually number 18,000. The planning proposals provide not only for new houses, schools, roads and sewage works but also for some 500 acres of public open spaces, including a 300 acre country park bounded on three sides by

Fenn Creek, the River Crouch and Clementsgreen Creek. There is already a twenty acre nature reserve at Woodham Fen, to the west of the development area, and it is pleasing to know that the County Council has plans to protect and enhance the natural environment.

Opposite to South Woodham Ferrers, on the south bank of the Crouch, is Hullbridge, a large bungalow settlement, yachting and fishing centre, complete with riverside inn and boatyards. Further along the river, on its north bank, beyond Stow Creek, is North Fambridge, a well-kept village with an eighteenth-century brick church. Across the river lies South Fambridge, now part of Ashingdon where, on 18th October 1016, the Danes under king Cnut defeated the English under king Edmund Ironside. This was an important battle, an agreement made soon after it giving Cnut all England except Wessex, which also accepted him as king after Edmund died in November 1016. It has been suggested that, as Cnut was also king of the Danes and the Norwegians, England might have remained part of a Scandinavian Empire if only the Normans had not arrived fifty years later. In such circumstances the history of the Battle of Ashingdon would have been more widely appreciated than it is at present. Not that twentieth-century Danes are ignorant of this connection between Denmark and England. Their generosity has enabled restoration to be carried out at the church that stands on the site of one built of stone and lime by Cnut for the souls of the slain.

From its hill the present church of St Andrew at Ashingdon, with certain of its features dating from about 1300, looks across to Canewdon, also on the south side of the Crouch. Here the medieval church of St Nicholas stands on another hill, its tall and massive tower, buttressed and battlemented, having apparently also served as a lighthouse. Across the marshes, on the far side of the river, is Bridgemarsh Island, separated from the north bank of the Crouch by a creek. At the creekside is Althorne whose Perpendicular church of St Andrew contains a brass to William Hyklott who, early in the sixteenth century, "paide for the werkemanship of the wall of this churche".

A little further along the north side of the Crouch is Creeksea where, at Creeksea Place, a caravan-camp has been established about the surviving part of a large early-

Elizabethan house whose date, 1569, is recorded on an original rainwater-head. All Saints church was rebuilt in 1878 by Frederic Chancellor, Diocesan Surveyor to the St Albans diocese (which then included Essex). He—to quote Pevsner—"indulges in the most curious surface effects of stone, with bits of flint, brick, and tile". Chancellor also let himself go in this way at Steeple, between Creeksea and the River Blackwater.

Adjoining Creeksea is Burnham-on-Crouch, 'the Cowes of the East Coast', a renowned yachting centre with its moorings, boat-building and repairing yards and chandlers, lively regattas and other yachting events. The importance of yachting in this small town is further emphasised by the presence here of five yacht clubs – Royal Corinthian, Royal Burnham, Crouch, Burnham Sailing Club, and United Hospitals' Sailing Club. Perhaps the most attractive feature of Burnham is the terrace of pleasant colour-washed houses along the Quay. The church, St Mary's, lies one mile north of the town. Its oldest feature is the undecorated Purbeck marble font, dating from about 1200.

At Wallasea Island, opposite Burnham, is the Essex yacht marina where one of the main divisions is boat building. The River Crouch flows past and eventually discharges to the sea between Ray Sands and Foulness Island.

It is the River Roach and its branching creeks that dissect much of the area south of the seaward end of the River Crouch, forming islands and isolated marshes. At the head of the River Roach and just north of Southend-on-Sea stands Rochford, an ancient market town whose centre has been declared a conservation area. South Street is particularly noteworthy for its old houses, some of Georgian red brick, others timber-framed, plastered and gabled. With its early-Tudor brick tower – large, tall and diapered; the church of St Andrew dominates that part of the town beyond the railway. Nearby is Rochford Hall, the converted remains of a sixteenth-century brick mansion. This is reputed to have been the birthplace of Henry VIII's second queen, Anne Boleyn, whose father, Sir Thomas Boleyn, was created Viscount Rochford in 1525. Later, in 1568, Richard Rich, first Baron Rich of Leez Priory, died there. He was Lord Chancellor for three years. Earlier he held the office of Chancellor of the Court of Augmentations at the Dissolution of the Monasteries, and many of the abbey lands "stuck to his fingers" (to use Fuller's wonderful expression).

Leaving Rochford and moving towards the coast, the Roach passes Great Stambridge (its partner survives only in the name of Little Stambridge Hall, a Georgian-fronted Tudor house). Here the church of St Mary and All Saints, with its Victorian interior, has slight evidence of Saxon origins. At Sutton, on the other side of the river, the church has Norman features and a fifteenth-century Essex weatherboarded belfry. Travelling towards remoter parts, the Roach passes Paglesham, separated from Wallasea Island by the waters of Paglesham Pool. This is a quiet region of halls, weatherboarded buildings and, at Paglesham Reach, yacht-building. The nave and chancel of St Peter's church are Norman and the arms of George III hang over the chancel arch, further reminders of former times. On the southern side of the river Barling is set around creeks and saltings, and south of it are the Wakerings, Little and Great, whose churches have Norman features. Beyond these villages are the islands – Potton, Rushley, Havengore, New England and Foulness. The Roach flows between Wallasea and Foulness Islands, its waters finally merging with those of the Crouch.

Unlike the River Roach and indeed many more of our rivers, the River Roding, though finally joining the mighty Thames, remains simply a slow and quiet stream for most of its course. With its source at Molehill Green, four miles north-west of Great Dunmow, "the trickling stream" (as the Roding was once called) often dries up in its earlier stages during the summer. Flowing in a general direction south, the river reaches Little Canfield and, passing under Stane Street, the Roman Road from Hertfordshire to Colchester, it travels on to Great Canfield. Here is the site of a motte-and-bailey castle whose mount is 275 feet across and 45 feet high. Nearby the church, St Mary's, with impressive Norman features, includes a thirteenth-century wall painting of the Virgin and Child seated, a work in red and yellow, the surviving colours, of which experts think very highly.

The church also houses several monuments to members of the Wiseman family who were associated with the village for several generations. There is a brass to John Wyseman (died 1558) and his wife, daughter of a Lord Mayor of London. John, who founded the Great Canfield line of the family, was knighted at the Battle of the Spurs (1513) and became one of the Auditors to Henry VIII. Edward Wiseman, another member of the Great Canfield family, slept on a pillow and couch carved out of a tree-trunk as penance for his failure to deliver in time a letter written by his master, Robert Devereux, second Earl of Essex, to Elizabeth I, pleading for mercy. Refusing to sleep in a bed, Wiseman is said to have suffered this punishment for forty-five years.

Leaving this small place, so rich in historical associations, the river enters 'windmill land' where the cluster of villages called 'the Rodings' lies. "As she [the River Roding] passeth", wrote an old historian, "she greeteth her daughters, all the Rodings." At High Roding church the nave, chancel and ironwork on the door date from the thirteenth century. Aythorpe Roding also has a church with thirteenth-century nave and chancel, only half a mile from which is a complete example of a post mill, the one recorded by Donald Smith in *English Windmills* as being the Essex post mill with the largest body.

The church at White Roding has a Norman nave with Roman brick quoins and a square Norman font, and barely a quarter of a mile from it the tower of the last tower mill to be built in Essex survives, the mill itself having ceased work nearly fifty years ago. Across the river, opposite White Roding, is Leaden Roding where the nave and chancel of St Michael's church are Norman. St Edmund's church at Abbess Roding, west of the river, has font, nave and chancel of the twelfth, fourteenth and fifteenth centuries respectively, though it has later features and was restored in 1867. There are monuments to Sir Gamaliel Capel, one of the eleven children of Sir Henry Capel (1537-1588) of Rayne Hall, Essex, and Little Hadham Hall, Hertfordshire, and to his youngest daughter Mildred. Also in this village, once the property of the abbesses of Barking, is Rookwood Hall, moated like so many Essex buildings.

On the other side of the river, St Margaret's at Margaret Roding probably claims what has been considered to be the greatest interest. Certainly this thick-walled little church has some Norman windows, a restored Norman doorway, and sixteenth-century plate, and it is nicely placed among trees, things of living beauty that so often outlive man and beast. South of Margaret Roding the river passes between two more of its 'daughters', Berners Roding, its small church in the Hall farmyard, on its east side, and Beauchamp Roding, its church standing alone in the fields, on the other.

Leaving the Rodings the river reaches Fyfield where the church, St Nicholas, has a Norman nave and a central crossing tower that was partly rebuilt last century. This village seems to have attracted a number of alert and enterprising parsons. Dr Anthony Walker, rector for thirty years towards the end of the seventeenth century endowed a schoolmaster in an effort to root out of the parish "as much as may be" atheism, ignorance, profanity and sin. Two hundred years later the then rector, Dr L. Elwyn Lewis, himself a keen cyclist, started short services for cyclists, the sermons being limited to five minutes duration and tea being provided at sixpence a head. About 800 cyclists attended the first of these services in 1899.

Passing under High Ongar bridge on the Ongar-Chelmsford road, the Roding enters a region where it is joined by the Cripsey Brook and several other tributaries. St Mary's church at High Ongar, with its ornate Norman doorway, stands opposite buildings that serve as reminders of coaching days. Chipping Ongar (usually referred to simply as Ongar) is next on the Roding's journey to the Thames. This town at the end of one of the Central Lines is proud of its Norman church, St Martin of Tours, which, though altered and added to, is of considerable historical interest. North-east of the church is the site of Ongar castle. This impressive Norman fortress was demolished long ago but the great mound survives, the remains of one stronghold of Count Eustace of Boulogne. One of William Duke of Normandy's most prominent supporters at the Battle of Hastings, he became the greatest lay baron in Essex (and also in Hertfordshire).

Flowing under the A113 road, the Roding passes between Stapleford Tawney and Stapleford Abbotts. The church at the first-named place received the attentions of the Victorians and has never been the same since. As if to compensate for this, the hall near the church is of Georgian red brick, while the Old

Rectory is of seventeenth to eighteenth-century brick. Stapleford Abbotts has an ugly church containing monuments and mural tablets to the Abdys of Albyns, the early seventeenth-century house which was partly destroyed by enemy action during the Second World War. Seated in Essex for over 250 years, the family included men who distinguished themselves in a number of different ways. Anthony Abdy, who died in 1640, was an alderman of the City of London, Sir Robert Abdy, a patriotic man of "unshaken integrity and remarkable humanity", represented Essex in Parliament for twenty-one years during the first half of the eighteenth century, and Edward Strutt Abdy, who died in 1846, was a fellow of Jesus College, Cambridge, who wrote on the U.S.A., where fittings of the family house were taken between the two world wars.

Meandering westwards, the river flows between Abridge and Theydon Mount. Abridge, a small thoroughfare settlement on a busy main road, has a small nineteenth-century brick church and three pubs – 'White Hart', 'Blue Boar', and 'Maltsters' Arms', the last-named weatherboarded. At Theydon Mount the little seventeenth-century red-brick church of St Michael stands on a hill, the main one of the village. The small chancel is crowded with monuments to the Smith family who lived at Hill Hall in whose grounds the church was built. An important early Elizabethan house, the mansion has been altered in many respects and has been administered by the Prison Commissioners as an open prison since 1952. Sir Thomas Smith, who built it in such a magnificent position, was a Saffron Walden man, the son of a sheep farmer. He acquired the Theydon Mount estate when he married his second wife, the widow of Sir John Hampden. At Cambridge, where he earned the description of "flower of the University", he had influenced Roger Ascham, the great classical scholar and tutor to Princess (later Queen) Elizabeth. By the time he died at the age of sixty-five in 1577 Sir Thomas was regarded as a real English gentleman who treated his tenants kindly and fairly and one who was learned in several subjects. His controversial political career, still the subject of argument, is another matter.

Twisting and turning, the Roding passes between Debden Station (Loughton) and the site of a Roman settlement, north-east of Woolston Hall. Loughton, an extensive residential area and modern shopping centre on the fringes of Epping Forest, has a station on the London Transport Central Line, a fact serving as a reminder that not far away the Roding crosses the Essex border and flows into Greater London, eventually to join the Thames.

Like the Roding, the Roman River is a quiet waterway. One of the lesser-known Essex rivers, it does not make a majestic entry to the sea through its own wide or busy estuary but joins the River Colne opposite Wivenhoe. Rising in farming country on the western side of Great Tey, noted for the great Norman crossing tower of St Barnabas's church, the Roman River flows under the railway and the A12 Roman road, passing Copford Place, an attractive white brick house, and then Copford Hall, a red-brick Georgian house, and, also at Copford, the remarkable Norman parish church of St Mary the Virgin whose twelfth-century wall paintings are considered to be of outstanding importance.

Continuing through a well-wooded stretch of countryside, the Roman River passes within a short distance of the grounds of Stanway Hall, site of Colchester Zoo. It then skirts Chest Wood before flowing within about half a mile of the northern edge of Abberton Reservoir. Made by damming the Layer Brook, this major public water supply reservoir is frequented by large numbers of wildfowl, particularly mallard and wigeon, between September and March (access for bird-watching is strictly limited to authorised members of the Essex Bird Watching and Preservation Society).

The Roman River next passes Donyland Wood, continuing below Fingringhoe church, a neat and attractive building, the nave Norman, the tower with horizontal bands of stone and flint. Below the church by the river is a disused tide mill, once driven by tidal water. Between here and its confluence with the Colne estuary the river flows through water meadows which, together with the woods already mentioned, and the Essex Naturalists' Trust Kingsford Bridge Marsh Reserve form part of the Roman River Valley Conservation Zone. Special protection for this area to the south of Colchester was first suggested by the Colchester Civic Society to whose members all who love the Essex countryside must surely be most grateful.

The people of Harlow, or at least those who enjoy outdoor activities of one kind or another, must be equally grateful to those who decided to develop the waterside area of the River Stort (really a type of navigation canal here) as an important feature of the town park. Making its appearance in the north-west of the county, the Stort is at first little more than a trickle of water. Not far from the Hertfordshire border it is associated with Clavering. Large and scattered, this attractive village includes the remains of the rectangular site of a castle built by Robert FitzWimarc, a Breton who, anticipating the Norman Conquest, served under both Edward the Confessor and the Conqueror as Sheriff of Essex.

Flowing more or less parallel with the Essex border, the Stort reaches Manuden, a charming village with timber-framed cottages near its large brick-floored church. This includes a memorial to Sir William Waad, Clerk of the Council to Elizabeth I and James I and builder of Battails (Battles) Hall, Manuden. Sir William's father, Armigel (Armagil), who died in 1568, was, according to his son's memorial, reputed to be the first Englishman to discover America. Styled 'the English Columbus', he did, in fact, sail to Cape Breton and Newfoundland in 1536.

South-east of Manuden is Stansted Mountfitchet (Stansted, as it is usually called), a growing town on the eastern side of the Stort. Its airport (or rather Government plans for its development) brought Stansted into the headlines a few years ago. The town was, however, already important in Norman times. The church of St Mary the Virgin has features of those early years, including the chancel arch and south doorway, but only remains of earthworks survive as evidence of the existence of the castle which dominated the early medieval town.

Further south the Stort crosses the border and flows through Bishop's Stortford in Hertfordshire. Later it forms a rough and ready natural boundary between "happy homely loving Hertfordshire" (to use Charles Lamb's description) and Essex. It flows to the west of Great Hallingbury, where the church has a Roman brick Early Norman chancel arch, and then Little Hallingbury, its church with a Norman doorway with Roman bricks. North-west of the church is Wallbury Camp, a thirty-one-acre Early Iron-Age hill-fort sited on a spur above

Spellbrook Lock on the Stort Navigation. Further along the Stort's course is Harlow, the new town dealt with in some detail elsewhere in this book. At Roydon, near the ruin of Nether Hall, the Colt family's early-Tudor manor house, a lane and track lead to the point where, at Rye House in Hertfordshire, the waters of the Stort merge with those of the Lea from Bedfordshire.

The River Lea (or Lee) runs along the remaining small portion of the Essex border before entering Greater London to join the Thames at Blackwall. By the banks of the Lea at Waltham Holy Cross (often called Waltham Abbey), in a busy industrial and residential area, are the remains of the great abbey founded in 1030 as a collegiate church of secular canons (it was later re-founded). A 120-foot long structure with massive arcade piers, triforium and clerestory, the Norman nave of the abbey church serves as parish church, its long use for this purpose having saved it from destruction after the Dissolution. The sixteenth-century west tower was added to mark this change from monastic to parochial use. Now the church is separated from the market square by a range of sixteenth-century timber-framed buildings. This includes the Welsh Harp Inn with its exposed timbers.

The Lee Valley Regional Park Authority, who are developing the first area in Britain to be selected as a Regional Park, recognize the section in the vicinity of the abbey as a great centre of general interest. Their plans for this area provide for a museum complex associated with local history and Lee Valley archaeology. This will interest many people, as should the tree nursery and arboretum, the indoor riding establishment and the angling centre, all of which will form part of the Waltham Abbey section of the park.

What, one wonders, would Izaak Walton have thought of an angling centre. We may be reasonably certain that he, author of that classic *The Compleat Angler*, who sat on the banks of the Lea more than three hundred years ago, would have approved of any scheme that encouraged people to enjoy the quiet pleasures of the waterside.

IV

THE GREAT COUNTY TOWNS

CHELMSFORD is not only the county town, the seat of local government for the whole of Essex, but also an important commerical, shopping, and residential centre, and an industrial town whose name is familiar in many parts of the world, largely through the activities of Marconi and other businesses.

The Romans were here, but evidence of their presence, like much of that relating to later periods, has been destroyed, allowed to disappear under modern buildings, or simply awaits discovery. Rivers divide this area almost at the centre of the county, and an important step in the development of the town was taken when, about 1100, Maurice, Bishop of London and Lord of the Manor of Chelmsford, built the historic bridge represented in the centre of the shield of the town's coat of arms, on which the two 'bars wavy' symbolize the ford of the River Chelmer, the source of Chelmsford's name. In recent years the development of the river valleys through the town has resulted in the creation of pleasant riverside walks from the town centre. In addition there are several playing fields and parks, including Central Park, whose lake, bowling green, tennis courts and children's playground, make it a valuable feature in the very heart of the town.

Chelmsford, recognizing the vital historical importance of this elegant structure, has scheduled John Johnson's late-eighteenth-century Stone Bridge, successor to the medieval bridge, for preservation as an ancient monument. Johnson, an architect, was surveyor for Essex from 1782 to 1812. Another of his works is the Shire Hall in Tindal Square, an outstanding building of white brick, faced with Portland stone, whose attractive features include three relief-plaques by John Bacon, R.A. in Coade's Artificial Stone. The fine County Room retains its rich and elaborate ceiling and frieze and elsewhere in the building there are portraits of Lords-Lieutenant of Essex and other pictures of local interest.

The original County Hall, erected in Duke Street in 1935 as the administrative headquarters of Essex, has been considerably extended in recent years. The Civic Centre at the corner of Duke Street and Coval Lane, now the administrative centre for the Chelmsford District, one of fourteen Districts into which Essex was divided at the reorganization of local government in 1974, was completed in 1962. The first phase of the Civic Centre scheme, the neo-Georgian Public Library, a two-storey building of honey-coloured brick with Portland stone dressings, was erected before the 1939-45 war. The second phase was finished after the war and includes the Civic Theatre, Council Chamber, and offices. Designed to seat some 550, the Civic Theatre caters for both professional and amateur companies. Another civic enterprise, the Chancellor Hall where dancing, wrestling, and other activities take place, is situated in the town centre close to Tindal Square.

People involved in the activities of Essex County Council, as well as those using facilities provided by the District Council and other interests, come to Chelmsford from all parts of the county and also from places further afield. The Cathedral Church of St Mary the Virgin, St Peter and St Cedd, in the heart of the county town, also attracts many folk. Rightly described as "a living monument to Chelmsford's history", this cathedral with a parish is a busy place. A Norman church is believed to have stood on the site, and fragments of work of that time have been detected in the walling of the tower. Rebuilding was certainly carried out early in the fifteenth century. Later the church suffered in the Civil War. In 1800 the nave roof collapsed after gravediggers had dug away the foundation of one of the pillars. Three years later it was rebuilt by John Johnson, whose name has already appeared in this chapter.

In 1914 a new diocese was created to contain "the County of Essex and that part of the County of Kent which lies north of the river Thames". Chelmsford parish church was chosen to be the cathedral, the place housing the seat (the throne or 'cathedra') of the Bishop of Chelmsford whose diocese is now the second largest in England (in terms of population). The

Bishop's throne, a fine example of modern wood carving, faces the statue of John Edwin Watts-Ditchfield, first Bishop of the diocese.

There is, of course, much else to see in Chelmsford Cathedral. But I would devote my limited space to a few of the features connecting modern Essex with earlier times. The chapel of St Cedd on the north side of the chancel and that of St Peter on the south, now used for celebrations of Holy Communion during the week and for services with small congregations, are living reminders of the earliest days of Christianity in Essex. St Cedd, Bishop of the East Saxons, who was sent to Christianize the people of Essex, built his chapel of St Peter-ad-murum at Bradwell-on-Sea in 654 AD. Still standing, it is now a place of pilgrimage. In 1964, the fiftieth anniversary of the founding of the diocese, a living flame was carried from this ancient chapel beside the sea to St Peter's Chapel in the cathedral where it is kept burning in an old Florentine lamp. The links between the cathedral and Bradwell are again emphasized by the presence of a carved figure of St Peter on the outside wall of the chapel bearing his name. This statue with St Peter dressed in modern fisherman's boots and holding a Yale key, is a symbol of the parts played by the cathedral in the everyday life of Essex.

Sport, one important factor in everyday life, is quite well provided for in Chelmsford. Melbourne Park Playing Field, the town's largest playing area, includes an athletic stadium, while Coronation Park, with its rugby pitches, is the home of Chelmsford Rugby Football Club. There are several other parks and playing fields whose facilities include pitches for football, hockey and cricket. Essex County Cricket Club, now (1976) celebrating its centenary, bought its ground at New Writtle Street, Chelmsford, as recently as 1965, many years after having played all its matches in festival weeks on grounds in different parts of the county. Nowadays about half the season's programme is played away from the Chelmsford ground in 'local weeks'. Essex has produced its share of Test cricketers, and it is pleasing to note that, in its centenary year, the club is appealing for £60,000 with which to build an indoor cricket school whose use by schools and youth teams will be encouraged.

When Essex County Cricket Club was founded in 1876 *The Chelmsford Chronicle: or, Essex Weekly Advertiser*, the first Essex newspaper, was already 112 years old. Its weekly announcements of sporting fixtures and other social activities must have attracted many of the nobility, gentry, tradesmen and farmers, for whom the editor wished to provide a public service. The *Essex Chronicle* and the *Chelmsford and Essex Weekly News* (to mention but two newspapers published in the county town) now cater for a much wider audience, playing a vital role in the life of a busy place whose record of industrial achievement is outstanding.

With its undoubted status as a real force in the industrial and commercial world, Chelmsford is delightfully English in a number of ways. It was here, for example, that Morris dancing was revived as recently as 1972. Now the Chelmsford Morris Side (who are unusual in that they admit ladies to membership) provide colourful entertainment and often, in doing so, raise worthwhile sums for charity. Dancing mainly Cotswold Morris dances, the lady members wear long wrap-around skirts whose colours match the ribbons of the men's bell pads. The men wear brown waistcoats bearing the golden eagle from the old Roman emblem for Chelmsford, a reminder of the town's past and some compensation, albeit small, for the shortage of historical remains.

Unlike Chelmsford, Colchester has preserved much of its past. Even so, it has much that is contemporary and it is certainly a place to enjoy. Its size seems right and the historic town centre above the River Colne stands apart from modern suburbs. The mixture of ancient and recent buildings is always interesting, sometimes whimsical. And Colchester seems to wear its past lightly, perhaps far too lightly, for as Philip Crummy points out in his booklet *Not only a matter of time* (1975): "There can be little doubt that Colchester is one of the handful of prime British archaeological sites whose rate of destruction through development, redevelopment and agriculture poses serious archaeological problems." From several points in the town one catches sight of trees and the surrounding countryside, and within a short distance of busy streets one may walk by the river as it passes slowly to the sea, only eight miles away.

Between the River Colne and the Roman River one can follow on foot ancient dykes and ramparts. Forming part of a great system of earthworks, they protected Camulodunum, the capital of the powerful Cunobelin (*circa* A.D. 5–40), the most famous king of the Belgic tribes in Britain. These Belgae, vigorous Iron Age peoples of mixed Celtic and Teutonic blood from north-east France and Belgium, used the heavy plough with share, made pottery on the wheel, produced beautiful metalwork, and struck coins. Excavations at Sheepen, one of two main occupation sites in Belgic Colchester (the other is Gosbecks), have brought to light pottery, coin moulds, and coins inscribed with CVNO for Cunobelinus and CAMV for Camulodunum. Examples of these finds may be seen in the Castle Museum.

The castle is the natural place from which to pursue the course of Colchester's history, for it stands above four vaults, the very foundations of the Temple of Claudius. This great building was erected by the Romans who, on invading Britain in A.D. 43, made Camulodunum their principal objective, and established on the ridge to the south-east the first *colonia* of veteran soldiers in A.D. 49–50. We cannot be sure how long Roman Colchester lasted, but the discovery of pagan Saxon pottery has led to the suggestion that it survived for a few decades after A.D. 410, the year in which Emperor Honorius told the British towns that they must in future look to their own defences, thus officially separating them from the Roman Empire.

The collections at the Castle Museum include coins, small objects, mosaic pavements, military tombstones, pottery and glass, fascinating evidence of the presence and activities of the Romans in Colchester. But the massive town walls are perhaps the most remarkable reminders of the Roman presence here. Built early in the second century A.D. and subsequently repaired on a number of occasions, they defended Colchester right up until the siege of 1648. After that event the parapets were demolished by command of Lord Fairfax, whose original letter to the Mayor of Colchester, ordering him to provide implements to demolish the walls and fortifications, is in the Essex Record Office.

The Roman walls are best seen along Park Folley, Priory

Street and Balkerne Lane. Visitors to the last-named place will find, at the crest of the hill, the ruins of the Balkerne Gate, the west gate of the Roman town. Once large and impressive and flanked by towers, it had four arched entrances, two wide ones for wheeled traffic, the narrower ones for pedestrians. Today from the terrace of the 'Hole in the Wall', the charming little public house that sits on the Roman wall above the Balkerne Gate, one may enjoy the magnificent view over the countryside to the north and imagine oneself a sentry of long ago. One is brought back swiftly to modern times when, looking round the immediate neighbourhood, one sees, standing behind the Balkerne Gate, the Mercury Theatre where plays, musicals, pantomimes and concerts have been staged since 1972. And who, when beholding here for the first time 'Jumbo', the enormous Victorian water tower standing above Tudor cisterns and bearing the name of a famous African elephant, could fail to be brought back to contemporary reality? But history soon takes over again, for just across the road from the Balkerne Gate a Romano-Celtic temple was discovered in 1975, bringing the number found at Colchester to eight, the largest single total for any place in England.

One must return to the museum for evidence of pagan Saxon occupation of Roman Colchester—pieces of pottery. In 1972 two pagan Saxon huts were excavated in Lion Walk. Close to this site stands Holy Trinity. Withdrawn from regular use as a place of worship in 1952, it was opened as a museum of agriculture in 1974. The west tower, with its small triangular headed doorway, is the only Anglo-Saxon (pre-Conquest) building in the town.

The remains of the keep of Colchester Castle, built (as already mentioned) on the site of the Roman Temple of Claudius, stand as evidence of the Norman presence in the town. Begun about 1080, the castle keep, the largest built by the Normans in England, was constructed of Roman bricks and dressed stones from ruins of Roman buildings, and septaria, compacted clay nodules quarried from the London Clays. Kentish ragstone was also used, as was white stone imported from Normandy in the twelfth century. Once almost twice as high as it now is, Colchester castle remained for many years a royal fortress largely in the gift of the king. According to the surviving copy of a document of 1101, Henry I granted 'both keep and castle' to Eudo de Rie, steward of William I and II and Henry I, who fought for the Conqueror at Hastings. Eudo remained Constable of Colchester Castle for twenty years and, like him, those who held the office for varying periods between 1120 and 1629 (when the castle was alienated from the Crown) were persons of distinction.

One of them, William de Lanvalei III, had taken part in the historic meeting at Bury St Edmunds, in neighbouring Suffolk, when the barons took their oath to seek the constitutional changes embodied in Magna Carta, the great charter of liberties granted by King John in 1215. Within the next year or two Colchester Castle was twice temporarily occupied by the French, and a little later that century it became a gaol, a purpose for which it continued to be used until 1835: A museum for more than a century and a War Memorial since 1920, the castle now stands surrounded by lawns and roses. But to those who know its history it is a grim survivor of less tolerant times, a constant reminder of the evils of intolerance.

Let us seek to remember as we walk here William Chivelyng, the Colchester tailor who, convicted of heresy in 1429, was burned before the castle. He was one of many such martyrs. Remember, too, the Catholics imprisoned here under Elizabeth I, the seventeenth-century Royalist prisoners, and many more. Few memorials have been raised to these men and women, but visitors will see in Colchester Castle a simple monument bearing the words: "James Parnell, Quaker, imprisoned for his faith and died here 1656, aged 19." This young man's death made him the first Quaker martyr, but not before he had written the memorable words:

"I charge you, profess no more in life than you seal [= practise]; preach the light in your lives and let it shine forth in your conversation."

Having recalled unhappy experiences of prisoners and martyrs who suffered there in more recent times, one remembers that it was Eudo de Rie, first Constable of the Castle, who founded St John's Abbey, where he is buried, in 1096. Dedicated to St John the Baptist, this Benedictine abbey was built outside the ancient town walls, by the Mersea Road. Only the fifteenth-century gatehouse, an ancient monument in the care of the Department of the Environment, remains, a vestige of the great and powerful house whose last abbot, John Beche, was hanged, having refused to recognize the supremacy of Henry VIII, who can only be regarded as one of a long line of monsters whose recent members include Hitler and Stalin. The abbey was dissolved and eventually the remains were sold to John Lucas, town clerk and lawyer. His descendant, Sir Charles Lucas, was shot in the castle bailey after the Siege of Colchester of 1648, during which the Lucas family house in the abbey grounds, a fortified strongpoint, was destroyed.

It was during the Siege that the great Norman church of St Botolph's Priory was battered down, leaving only parts of the west front and the nave, ruins now cared for by the Department of the Environment. Standing about 350 yards south of the castle and only a short distance outside the Roman town wall, St Botolph's Priory was founded between 1093 and 1100 on the site of an earlier church. The first house of Augustinian Canons in England, St Botoloph's was granted many privileges by Pope Paschal II, but it remained a comparatively small and poor foundation. In the sixteenth century, at the suppression of the monasteries, St Botolph's Priory Church (or, at least, its nave) was preserved for parochial use, the rest of the priory and its possessions being granted to Sir Thomas Audley, Lord Chancellor. During the following century, with the Priory church destroyed during the Siege, the parish was united with that of All Saints', a situation that continued until 1836-8 when the present church of St Botolph was built in white brick in the 'Norman' style.

The modern St Botolph's was the first entirely new church to be built in Colchester since the Middle Ages. Fortunately for those with time and patience many of the older churches remain, often restored, modernized, or declared redundant, but all yielding, from clues provided by the buildings themselves, their monuments and their histories, something of the town's past and the lives of departed citizens.

Reference has already been made to Holy Trinity. Now a museum, All Saints', in its little churchyard opposite the castle, embodies a Norman wall and has a few epitaphs. St Giles's, now occupied by the Colchester Freemasons, was founded by the Mersea Road, probably for the tenants and servants of St

John's Abbey. Later, as the chapel of the Lucas family, it became the burial place of Sir Charles Lucas and Sir George Lisle, whose black marble memorial refers to their being "in cold blood barbarously murdered", a stark reference to their execution after the siege of 1648 and a sad reminder of the bitter results of civil war.

On East Hill the church of St James the Great has architectural details dating from the twelfth and thirteenth centuries. Among later features is a monument to Arthur Winsley, alderman and cloth merchant, who founded the almshouses in Winsley Square, off Old Heath Road, in 1727.

The oldest parts of the present St Leonard's-at-the-Hythe, the much restored parish church of the Hythe, the port of Colchester, are of the mid-fourteenth century. At the time of the Siege of 1648 this church was a Royalist stronghold, but eventually it was taken by the Parliamentary forces who held there a thanksgiving "for ye victory in the north". St Martin's in West Stockwell Street, with its twelfth century tower, was damaged in the Siege. Considered to be architecturally one of the most interesting churches in the town, it has been used as a drama centre since 1958.

One cannot for long forget the past in Colchester, a fact which is brought to mind in St Peter's on North Hill where the large collection of brasses and other memorials includes a broken marble slab commemorating Sir William Campion, a Royalist officer killed at the beginning of the Siege. The medieval church of St Mary's-at-the-wall, just east of Balkerne Lane, was virtually destroyed in the Siege when it became a Royalist stronghold. Only the stump of the fifteenth-century tower survived to be embodied in later work. A large monument to John Rebow survives from the early eighteenth century when his son, Sir Isaac Rebow, the wealthy cloth merchant and M.P., contributed to the cost of rebuilding the church. A family of Flemish extraction, the Rebows contributed to the life of Colchester for many years.

Flemish and other refugees, principally weavers who manufactured the woollen cloths known as 'Bays and Says', had arrived in Colchester late in the sixteenth century. Known locally as Dutch, they contributed magnificently by their skill and industry to the town's prosperity during the following two centuries, service so beautifully commemorated in a fine stained glass window in the council chamber of the town hall. The Dutch Bay Hall, where regulations for the production of the cloths were introduced and enforced, was at the top of High Street close to the area in which some of the weavers lived.

This so-called Dutch Quarter is situated to the west of the castle grounds, lying between Castle Park, West Stockwell Street, High Street and St Peter's Street. It is an area of winding streets where, well before the refugees had arrived, order had been achieved without the sacrifice of informality. The buildings, half-timbered and plastered houses included, display attractive proportions and a wealth of interesting detail, and often a narrow street is blessed with a distant view. What a treasure this is in the very heart of a modern town! And what fine and commendable enterprise was brought to fruition when Colchester Borough Council restored some forty houses here, a scheme for which they won a Civic Trust award.

From the Dutch Quarter it is but a short walk along High Street to The Hollytrees. One of many survivors of the Georgian period, this red-brick building of three storeys struck Pevsner as the best eighteenth-century house of Colchester. Now a museum housing collections of eighteenth-century and nineteenth-century objects, costume and needlework, the house was built in 1718-9, the floor-boards of the earlier half-timbered building being used in its construction. Within seven or eight years of its completion the owner of the new house died, her niece married a wealthy merchant, moved to The Hollytrees, was widowed, and then remarried to become the wife of Charles Gray. This native of Colchester, a lawyer and antiquary, represented the town in parliament from 1742-55 and 1761-80. He is remembered locally for his care and restoration of the castle and its grounds, but his living memorial must surely be the holly trees he planted "in ye middle of March" 1729 and which are still growing in the front garden of The Hollytrees.

The Minories, on the other side of the street, is a late Georgian house with a rear wing dating from the early sixteenth century. Now an art gallery, it was the home of Thomas Boggis, a bay-maker, who, in 1776 (the year he was mayor of the town), rebuilt the main part of the house. Boggis provided employment for a large number of men and women, the cardmakers, spinners, weavers, fullers, beaters and rowers, whose labours eventually resulted in the conversion of raw wool into cloth. The son of Peter Devall, his manager, became the last of the Colchester bay-makers. Such is the intrusion of the twentieth century that a road leading to the bus park and a multi-storey car park now runs alongside The Minories, occupying the site of the former kitchen garden, stables and outhouses.

Beyond the entrance to the bus park is East Hill House, a fine example of early eighteenth-century simplicity with a slightly later top storey. It was the home of George Wegg, the Tory attorney, to whom Isaac Boggis, baymaker, son of an East Hill baker and a Dutch mother, and father of Thomas Boggis (just mentioned), left a mourning ring. Many buildings in East Hill, North Hill, Crouch Street, and other thoroughfares display imposing Georgian frontages, fine proportions and elegant porticos. In High Street the George Hotel, with its eighteenth-century front and attractive cast-iron balcony, faces the Red Lion Hotel, a remarkable timber-framed building whose exposed front timbers date from about 1500, thus creating a situation so characteristic of Colchester.

The town's Georgian houses are symbols of wealth created largely in the cloth trade during the previous century. This trade, damaged during the siege, declined even more as the result of the Napoleonic Wars at the end of the Georgian period. But these same wars brought a garrison to Colchester and the town has been an important military centre ever since.

The Napoleonic camp was demolished long ago, but its burial ground is the site of the timber-framed and weather-boarded Camp Church (or Garrison Chapel), the only surviving relic of the barracks established to the south of the old town in 1856. War and the role of the army have both changed considerably since then, but there are times when events of the past are called vividly to mind through traditional ceremonies at the modern barracks. Such an occasion was the visit to the 1st Battalion Worcestershire and Sherwood Foresters Regiment of Princess Anne, Colonel-in-Chief. Just returned from Northern Ireland and undertaking their first tour of duty in Colchester, the soldiers were accompanied by

Derby XXII. The first ram in the long succession of official mascots bearing the name Derby had been acquired by the 95th Regiment of Foot during the Indian mutiny in 1858, at a time when industrial and urban development was beginning to bring about the growth of Colchester.

An important contributory factor in this Victorian expansion was the arrival of the railway from London in 1843. Some details of industrial growth are included in another chapter, but we must here remind ourselves that during Queen Victoria's long reign the population of Colchester was doubled. Certain of the town's Victorian buildings are now among its most prominent landmarks. Jumbo, the massive water tower, has already been mentioned. Another, the tower of the town hall in High Street, is seen in full sunlight as a delightful tribute to Queen Victoria who saw the designs and gave permission for it to be named in her honour. The town hall, whose foundation stone was laid in 1898, was opened early in 1902. Linking the Victorian and Edwardian eras, it replaced the second town hall of 1843 and the earlier Moot Hall. Its stained glass windows and other features illustrate the town's history, including not only personalities such as St Helena, patron saint of Colchester, and Claudius, founder of the Roman colony, but also Boadicea (Boudicca), who burnt the town down in A.D. 60-1.

The tall spire of the Lion Walk United Reformed Church dominates the immediate area and serves as a landmark far beyond it. Replacing the eighteenth-century "round meeting house", the present church opened in 1863. The congregation having first assembled in the 1640s, it claims to be the oldest non-conformist church in Colchester. Other buildings exist to emphasize that religious activity, a vital feature of life in the town, continued to develop in Victorian times. The Roman Catholic church of St James-the-Less, in Priory Street, dates from 1837, the first year of Victoria's reign, and then, at intervals, other places of worship appeared: Spurgeon Memorial Chapel, Artillery Street (where Charles Haddon Spurgeon, the great preacher, was converted); Headgate United Reform Church, Chapel Street; All Saints', Shrub End; St Michael's, Mile End; St John's, Ipswich Road; St Paul's Belle Vue Road.

In addition, there was much restoration and rebuilding of

churches, and in 1882 the Salvation Army commenced their activities in the town, bringing music and, above all, the Word of God to people in the streets. By 1900 expansion, growing commercial pressures, and rebuilding had brought great changes to the town centre, particularly the High Street. Business and professional men now preferred to live in the suburbs and not over shop or office. After the First World War large new suburbs appeared at Lexden, Mile End, and Old Heath. By the outbreak of the Second World War motor traffic was causing problems, areas were being cleared in the old town for use as car parks, and chain stores had invaded the High Street. When peace returned there was much building, particularly of housing estates. Motor traffic increased and the old town lost much of its ancient peace and atmosphere.

But Colchester has shown an amazing ability to cope with changing circumstances, accommodating the new and retaining much of the old. As we have seen, it has put a number of its old parish churches to other uses. In this post-war reorganis-ation of the central parishes, St Nicholas's in High Street, whose tall spire was such a notable feature of the town's skyline, was pulled down, its bells going to St Martin's Church in the new town of Basildon, its mural memorials, vane, organ and other furnishings to other churches in Colchester.

New places of worship have appeared, among them the red-brick church of St Cedd at Shrub End, with its nave designed for use as a parish hall, and, much more recently, St Margaret's, Berechurch, "the first Anglican do-it-yourself church of Colchester", the result of four years of hard work by the parishioners themselves. Like St Margaret's, with its copper pyramid-shaped roof, the church of Jesus Christ of Latter Day Saints in Straight Road is of striking appearance. A building whose interesting shape is enhanced by a tall angular spire, this church was built during the 1960s by six young men working full time and many other members working in their free time. At that time the Seventh Day Adventists replaced the Gospel Hall in North Station Road by a new church, and in 1973 the Salvation Army's new citadel was opened in Butt Road. These events must surely indicate that Colchester is not only a healthy and active centre of religion but also a place from which spiritual values have not been completely ousted in our noisy hurried age.

Many Colcestrians, having long appreciated and quietly enjoyed their town's importance as a religious, cultural and historical centre, must have seen the opening of the University of Essex on an attractive site two miles to the east of the centre of Colchester as some kind of compensation for the fact that "Britain's oldest recorded town" is not *the* county town. It was October 1964 when the university admitted its first students and July 1967 when its first degrees were awarded at a congregation presided over by its Chancellor, Lord Butler of Saffron Walden.

Set in Wivenhoe Park, some 200 acres of well wooded, undulating country beside the River Colne, the teaching, office and laboratory buildings are planned in a continuous series of cellular units, residential accommodation being in tower blocks on the main site and in low-rise blocks of flats near to it. Some rude words have been used from time to time to describe these buildings whose erection in the eighteenth-century park where Constable painted (his picture of Wivenhoe Park now hangs in the National Gallery of Art in Washington) is occasionally seen as something of an intrusion.

However, it will be by the quality and achievements of its students that the university will eventually be judged. Certainly the academic plan, with its fresh approaches to teaching and to university life, has aroused much interest, as have the developing Schools of Comparative Studies, Physical Science, Social Studies, and Mathematical Studies, the Department of Language and Linguistics, and the Computing Centre. Let us hope that the university staff and students will find Wivenhoe Park as pleasing and inspiring a place as did Mary Rebow who lived there 200 years ago. To her it was "one of the most pleasing pictures in England".

V

TOWNS, VILLAGES AND CHURCHES

MANY ESSEX towns and villages are discussed in other chapters of this book, but I am conscious that others must receive attention if my portrait of the county is to be anything like a satisfactory one. I propose here, then, to suggest excursions from Chelmsford, the county town, that will enable active readers and armchair travellers alike to fill many gaps in our survey of places of interest.

Travelling to the north-west corner of Essex on the A130 road from Chelmsford, one may experience something more of the county's historic past by taking the minor road to the left and visiting Pleshey where earthworks of the mount and bailey of an important Norman castle and of the Norman town enclosure are well-preserved together with a fine fourteenth-fifteenth-century brick bridge.

The story of Pleshey begins with Geoffrey de Mandeville who, after the Norman Conquest, was rewarded by William of Normandy with the gift of a number of estates, including 12,000 acres around the stronghold of Pleshey in the centre of Essex. His grandson, who bore the same name and was a powerful baron (many say *the* most powerful of the barons in Essex), was made Constable of the Tower of London and first Earl of Essex by King Stephen. Active in this way to secure support in his struggle against Henry I's daughter Matilda, another claimant to the throne, Stephen was equally active when he discovered that de Mandeville was "running with the fox and hunting with the hounds". Deprived of Pleshey Castle and other possessions, de Mandeville was set free, being killed when fighting against Stephen in 1144.

De Mandeville's second son, Geoffrey, became the second earl, the estates being restored to him. He was succeeded by his brother, William, the third earl, who made his mark as ambassador to the Emperor Frederick and as Chief Justiciar. His death without issue brought the direct line to an end in 1190. Eventually the title of fourth Earl of Essex was bestowed on Geoffrey FitzPeter, husband of the granddaughter of the first Earl's sister Beatrix. The new earl became one of the five judges of the King's Court while Richard I was on crusade and later he was appointed Chief Justiciar. Succeeding him in 1213, his eldest son, Geoffrey, assumed the surname of Mandeville. He became a member of the committee of twenty-five appointed by the barons to hear complaints that might arise from King John's failure to carry out the promises contained in Magna Carta, if necessary compelling the king to observe the charter by seizing his castles and lands. When it became obvious that John had no intention of accepting that Magna Carta was permanently binding, Geoffrey took arms against him, in the interests of liberty and good faith. On Christmas Eve, 1215, the king's forces besieged Pleshey Castle, plundering, destroying and killing for miles around. On his death in 1216 (King John died the same year), Geoffrey was succeeded by his brother William, but when he died without issue eleven years later the direct line ended once more.

William's nephew, Humphrey de Bohun, son of the Earl of Hereford, became first Earl of Essex of the Bohun line. The earldom remained with this family until the death in 1373 of the sixth Earl whose daughters, Eleanor and Mary, shared the Bohun estates. It was Eleanor who married Thomas of Woodstock, Duke of Gloucester and youngest son of Edward III. At the age of twenty-five the Duke averted the landing of French and Spaniards at Dover and captured eight Spanish ships off Brest. The following year he dispersed insurgents in Essex. But his opposition to Richard II, whom he threatened with the fate of Edward II, who was brutally treated and murdered, led to his undoing. For, in 1397, Richard arrested him at Pleshey whence he was taken to Calais. There he died, probably murdered, at the age of forty-two. Three years before his death 'Uncle Gloucester' (he was indeed Richard's uncle) had founded at Pleshey a college of nine chaplains on a site south of the parish church. Time passed and the day came when the castle was in ruins, but perhaps it would be kindest to leave Pleshey at this point, return to the A130 road, and travel to Great Dunmow.

One of 440 places of settlement mentioned in Domesday, Great Dunmow had several watermills in Norman times. It became a borough in 1555, its first charter of incorporation being granted that year, and had a market twenty years later. Today Dunmow is a busy town whose shops and inns cater for resident and visitor alike. The large restored church of St Mary, with features of the fourteenth and fifteenth centuries, is at Churchend.

By turning off the A130 road and on to the B1057, one may travel to Finchingfield, the most visited and photographed place in the entire county. Appropriately in this 'picture-book' village, the church of St John, its square tower Norman and its rood screen most elaborate, lies on a hill. Nearby is the former guildhall (about 1500), one of many buildings whose varying heights and types create a delightfully informal atmosphere, one in which the village pond and the green are vitally essential features. The completely renovated post mill, with its brick roundhouse, stands on a mound above the road, an interesting example of the oldest type of windmill. Not far away is the Round House, a thatched hexagonal cottage built as a model cottage in the late eighteenth century.

One mile north-west of Finchingfield is Spains Hall, long the home of the Ruggles-Brise family. This sixteenth-century house of red brick with stone dressings was originally the home of the Kemps who had lived in an earlier house on the site. The family, whose chapel is in Finchingfield church, acquired Spains Hall when Nicholas Kemp married Margery, daughter of Richard de Ispania. Nicholas' descendant, William Kemp, who died in 1628, is remembered as one who remained silent for seven years as a penance (he had unjustly accused his wife of being unfaithful).

Spains Hall passed to Mary Kemp when her brother died without issue. In 1727 she married into the Dyer family who, thirty-three years later, sold Spains Hall to Samuel Ruggles, a wealthy clothier of Bocking. At his death the house passed to his nephew, Thomas Ruggles (died 1813), champion of poor agricultural workers in northern Essex and lifelong friend of Arthur Young, agriculturalist and writer. Thomas Ruggles' eldest son John succeeded him, assuming the name of Ruggles-

Brise. Great distinction was brought to this name earlier this century by Sir Evelyn Ruggles-Brise, 'Founder of Borstal', who, in the words of an inscription at the original Borstal: "determined to save the young and careless from a wasted life of crime".

Beyond Great Dunmow, on the A130, is Thaxted, "a little mercate towne", as William Camden described it, "seated very pleasantly upon an high rising hill." Visible for miles around, the church stands high up at the northern end of the town. "The Cathedral of Essex", as it was often called, this great church of St John Baptist, Our Lady and St Laurence (the patron saint of the cutlers) is essentially the church of a wealthy medieval community. The dates of its building (1340-1510) are those of a period when the cutlery industry made Thaxted a successful and prosperous place. There are many points of interest in what Sir John Betjeman so rightly calls "a joyful and uplifting church". The graceful stone spire with its flying buttresses is most attractive, while the lightness of the interior, largely the result of the amount of clear glass, is quite delightful.

There is no doubt that the long and devoted service of Conrad Noel (vicar, 1910-42) resulted in much being done for Thaxted church. This "socialist vicar", who created a sensation by hoisting the red flag in the church, should also be remembered for the complete sincerity with which he proclaimed the Social Gospel, his revival of a rich liturgical tradition, and his deep love for everyone and everything connected with his church. His wife Miriam played her part, too, restoring Morris dancing in the town and bringing the dancers into church. In transforming, as he himself put it, "this museum of the immediate past into a fragrant shrine of God for the everyday use of His people", Conrad Noel was also helped by his great friend Gustav Holst, the composer, who lived in Thaxted for several years. Later the Reverend Jack Putterill maintained much of the tradition established by his father-in-law.

Thaxted has a number of timber-framed and overhanging houses, but the fifteenth-century guildhall, at the top of Town Street, makes a lasting impression. Restored at a cost of £65,000, it was reopened early in 1976 by the Countess of Dartmouth, United Kingdom chairman for 1975 European

Architectural Heritage Year. The ground floor is an open market-house, on the first floor is the council chamber where the business of the town was conducted, and above it is the room used as a school from about 1613. From the Bull Ring one sees two rows of almshouses in the churchyard. In 1975 restoration work on these buildings earned the trustees one of the three Civic Trust European Architectural Heritage Year certificates awarded in Essex. Beyond the modernized alms-houses stands the windmill, a tower mill, lone survivor of Thaxted's five mills. Built in 1804, and worked until 1912, it is being repaired by volunteers.

Like Thaxted, the market town of Saffron Walden, further up the A130 road, has a large and magnificent parish church. Dedicated to St Mary the Virgin, it is the largest and the finest parish church in the whole of Essex. Certainly it is considered to be one of the finest examples of Perpendicular work in England. During recent years much attention has been paid to restoration. Metal rods have been inserted to prevent further trouble with the fifteenth to sixteenth-century roofs, the nave roof has been painted and restored, and the spire has been dealt with. Situated on the same elevated site as the church are the remains, the flint-rubble core, of the walls of the keep of the Norman castle which served as capital residence of the de Mandevilles, Earls of Essex.

Geoffrey de Mandeville, first Earl, founded a priory, which became an abbey in 1190, towards the western end of Saffron Walden. This Benedictine abbey was given, as one of a number of rewards, by Henry VIII to Sir Thomas Audley (later Lord Audley of Walden), Speaker of the Parliament whose approval of the appropriate Acts permitted the suppression of the monasteries. Having destroyed much of the place, Audley converted the remainder into a house where he died in 1544 (his black marble tomb is in Saffron Walden church). Lord Audley's daughter Margaret brought the house to the Howard family, having married the fourth Duke of Norfolk. He was beheaded for intriguing with Mary, Queen of Scots, and the first Audley End house passed to his son, Thomas Howard, who later became Lord Howard, Earl of Suffolk, Lord Chamberlain, and Lord High Treasurer of England.

It was this Earl of Suffolk, later to be disgraced, who built the great stately mansion, of which the present house is only part (and a restored and partially rebuilt part) between about 1603 and 1616. The building and its furniture was supposed to have cost £200,000, and King James to have declared: "This house is too large for a king, but it might do for a Lord Treasurer!" Audley End mansion did, in fact, pass into royal ownership when the third Earl of Suffolk sold it to Charles II. After thirty-two years of royal use, much of it only occasional, the house was conveyed to the fifth Earl of Suffolk in 1701. Then followed a sad period when total demolition of this last and greatest Essex house of the courtyard type was considered. Fortunately there arrived on the scene the creator of the Audley End we now know, Sir John Griffin Griffin (later to become the first Lord Braybrooke), who had inherited the property from his aunt, Elizabeth, Countess of Portsmouth, great-grand-daughter of the third Earl of Suffolk. Lord Howard, as Lord Braybrooke was usually called, spent £100,000 on the building, rebuilding, adding, reconstructing, and redecorating. In replanning the gardens, he found time to erect a tall column bearing an inscription to the memory of his benefactress, Lady Portsmouth. The house continued to be the residence of the family until 1941 when the seventh Lord Braybrooke died. Now this splendid Jacobean mansion, in its extensive and beautiful park by the River Cam, is the property of the nation, a treasure that all who are interested in our country and its history must surely visit on more than one occasion.

North-west of Saffron Walden at Little Chesterford, the Cam-side village on the A130 road, the Manor House includes a wing which is the earliest existing domestic building in Essex. Built of flint rubble and oolite early in the thirteenth century, this thick-walled wing is probably the complete original manor house. A timber-framed hall was added during the fourteenth century and another wing the following century.

Nearer the Cambridgeshire border, the large village of Great Chesterford, now an important centre of agrochemical research, became the site of a Roman fort after the Boudiccan rebellion. Later a Roman town was developed and walled about the beginning of the fourth century. Among the fascinating objects found here are the enormous 'scythe-blade' and fifty-two-inch cropping shears. It has been suggested that the former may indicate that experimentation was being carried on with some kind of reaping machine (one named the *Vallus* is mentioned by Pliny), while the shears, used to provide a smooth close finish to woollen cloth, must have come from a wool mill.

The A12 road from Chelmsford to Colchester, the great centre of Roman Essex, leads first to the attractive village of Boreham, its church of St Andrew with Norman central tower. New Hall was Henry VIII's Beaulieu, his 'beautiful place', but little of his large quadrangular mansion remains. The New Hall of today, a convent for many years, dates mainly from 1573 when the Earl of Sussex made alterations to the building. Boreham House, now Ford's Agricultural Equipment Training Centre, was built in 1728 for Benjamin Hoare, youngest son of the banker, and altered in 1812. An imposing building, it is obviously put to good use by a company that has contributed much to the industrial achievements of Essex.

Hatfield Peverel, considered by some people to be un-interesting, possesses one of the county's numerous living links between past and present. For the parish church of St Andrew is the nave of the church of the Benedictine priory, a cell of St Albans Abbey, which existed here for many years.

The modern road towards Colchester avoids Witham, but this growing town, with its new factories and housing, re-members that, before the coming of the by-pass, its High Street had been the main road from Roman times. At Chippinghill in Witham there are ancient houses around the little triangular green and the large flint church here is largely fourteenth century. Even older were the lines of King Edward the Elder's entrenchments, lines put down in the tenth century and practically obliterated by the railway nine centuries later.

The A12 also by-passes Kelvedon whose old houses and hostelries recall the days when travellers were glad to break their journeys here. A little evidence of Norman work is seen in the church of St Mary the Virgin where work of the thirteenth, fourteenth and sixteenth centuries is more abund-ant. A mile from Kelvedon is the pictureseque village of Feering. The church here has some good Tudor brickwork and, in its little Lady chapel, an altar made of stone from four destroyed monasteries and a lovely figure of the Virgin and Child found headless near the site of Colne Priory at Earls Colne and restored by a local craftsman.

This church should surely be a place of pilgrimage for all who love and enjoy the works of John Constable, 'the natural painter', for it was the Reverend Walter Wren Driffield, resident curate here for fifty years, who baptized the newly born child of Golding and Ann Constable, a child whose weak condition must have made them gravely anxious as to his chances of surviving. But survive he did and, thanks to the loving care of a twentieth-century rector, the *Risen Christ* John Constable painted for Manningtree in 1822 now hangs in Feering church. What a wonderful memorial to a dedicated country curate and his friend the great painter of the countryside who died within nine years of one another.

At the junction of the A12 with Stane Street (A120), and at a point west of Colchester, subject of part of another chapter, is Marks Tey. Here the tower of St Andrew's church has the top two stages and battlements of vertical weatherboarding. Also of oak, the octagonal font is of the fifteenth century.

Between Chelmsford and Billericay on the B1007 road is Stock, a pretty and pleasing village with a long green. The church has a fine wooden belfry tower and a brass to Richard Twedye, a justice of the peace of Boreham who died in 1574, having "served well against the Ingleshe foes in foren landes and eke at home". He founded the almshouses near the church which were rebuilt late in the seventeenth century. A bit further from the church stands Stock Tower Mill, one of the mills maintained by Essex County Council. Built at the very end of the eighteenth century, it was once one of three windmills standing in the same field.

Billericay, a growing residential town, has a long history. The Romans were here and a market existed in the fifteenth century. The long High Street has some interesting houses, including Burghstead Lodge, often thought of as the town's best house, and Chantry House, now a restaurant, part of a larger house where the Pilgrim Fathers are said to have assembled before embarking for America. This is according to tradition, as is the belief that the house was the home of Christopher Martin, the miller who, together with his brother-in-law and their servant, chartered the *Mayflower* and formed a company to emigrate to New England.

Across the road is the church, a chapel-of-ease in Martin's time and until the parish was formed in 1844, when Billericay had already outgrown its parent parish of Great Burstead. The low brick tower dates from about 1500, most other features being much later.

South of Billericay and the western side of Basildon, the subject of part of another chapter, lies Horndon-on-the-Hill, a hilltop village, as its name suggests, close to the industrial area of Thurrock. Carefully restored in 1969 by the John Poley Trust and once more open on the ground floor, the fine early-sixteenth-century market house is evidence of Horndon's earlier importance and prosperity. With large flocks of sheep on the Thames-side marshes, it was inevitable that Horndon market should deal largely in wool. The reduction of the flocks of marshland sheep in the sixteenth century meant the decline of Horndon and its wool market had ceased to function by 1594.

The mostly Early English church of St Peter and St Paul is another reminder of earlier times and so is the fifteenth-century timbered Bell Inn. The mere mention of this ancient hostelry conjures up pictures of past generations enjoying themselves, transacting business, plotting or merely gossiping. It also brings to mind one of the most frightful episodes of our not too distant past, the burning of Protestants during the Marian Reaction when the ill-advised Queen Mary set about restoring papal authority in England. For it was behind the Bell Inn that the burning took place of Thomas Higbed, a local farmer who was arrested in 1555, tried and condemned for heresy. "Do what ye will", he told his judges, "you will do no more than God will permit you to do and with what measure you measure to us, look for the same at God's Hands." Higbed was one of some three hundred who perished during the Marian persecution. Like all others who have lost their lives in attempting to resist persecution, they call to us three simple words: Dying we live!

Mary's successor, Elizabeth I, visited the house which stood on the site of the present Arden Hall, north-east of Horndon church, until about 1730. She spent the night there in 1588 after reviewing troops assembled at Tilbury when a Spanish invasion was feared.

A reminder of Elizabeth's repudiation of the papacy and the introduction of savage laws against Catholics (all priests and all who sheltered them were liable to be hanged as traitors) occurs as one follows the A12 road in a south-westerly direction from Chelmsford. For it was while living in the household of the Dowager Lady Petre at Ingatestone Hall that John Paine, the only priest to be executed in Essex under Elizabeth, was betrayed by George Elliott, the apostate spy who later betrayed Edmund Campion. Convicted on Elliott's evidence of uttering treasonable words against the queen, Paine, a much-loved man whose innocence was generally accepted locally, was hanged, drawn and quartered at Chelmsford on 2nd April, 1582.

One is even more sharply reminded of the religious struggles and persecutions of Tudor Essex at Brentwood, close to the boundary with Greater London. Here, in Shenfield Road, stands the William Hunter Memorial. Hunter, a young Protestant apprentice, was a victim of Queen Mary's attempt to impose (some say restore) the Catholic faith. Reported to Anthony Browne, the devout Catholic judge who lived at Weald Hall and was later knighted, by Thomas Wood, vicar of South Weald, Hunter was tried in London and condemned to death. Edmund Bonner, Bishop of London, having failed to get the prisoner to recant, Hunter was sent back to Brentwood where, on 26th March, 1555, he was burned "at the town's end where the butts stood", a site considered to be in Ingrave Road, opposite Brentwood School Chapel. It makes a sad commentary on the worldly affairs of mere mortals to state that Bonner, who was himself imprisoned on several occasions, was eventually deprived of his bishopric and died in the Marshalsea Prison.

Apart from his persecution of Protestants and the pursuit of activities bringing him wealth and social standing, Browne founded "the Grammar School of Anthony Browne, Serjeant at Law, in Brentwood, in the County of Essex", now known as Brentwood School. In October 1557 he bought the land where School House and the Old School now stand, and four hundred years later, on 30th October, 1957, the school was visited by the Queen and Prince Philip, an occasion on which her Majesty opened the new Science School, naming it the Queen's Building.

Like Browne's school, Brentwood has grown considerably during the past four centuries, but it has preserved among its modern houses, shops, and factories, relics of its past. In High Street are the remains of the Chapel of St Thomas the Martyr. Founded by the monks of St Osyth in or about 1221, it was intended largely for pilgrims using the ferry at Tilbury on their way to or from Canterbury where miracles were being wrought at the tomb of St Thomas. It is said that it was from this chapel in Brentwood that, in 1232, Hubert de Burgh, great patriot and once powerful Chief Justiciar, was dragged by Henry III's Steward of the Royal Household and troops. Taken in complete violation of sanctuary and removed to the Tower of London, he was returned to the chapel at Brentwood, surrendering to besieging troops when the forty days grace allowed by sanctuary ended. Imprisoned in the Tower and Devizes Castle, de Burgh was again accused of many crimes. Acquitted, he lived in retirement until 1243.

Part of another troubled life, that of Catherine of Aragon, first Queen of Henry VIII, was passed in Brentwood. The hunting lodge where she lived is in London Road. Known as the Moat House, it is now a hotel. There are many other places where the traveller may find rest and refreshment in and around the town. One of the most famous is the 'White Hart' in Brentwood High Street. A fine old coaching inn with courtyard and windowed gallery, it links the present with the time when thirty-two horse-drawn long distance coaches passed through the town.

Our fifth and final journey from Chelmsford follows at first the A122 road in a more or less westerly direction. Then, passing through High Ongar and turning off the main road, Greensted is reached. Sometimes called in the old manner Greensted-juxta-Ongar, this attractive village has long been and must surely remain a place of pilgrimage. For its church, St Andrew's, is the oldest wooden church in England and probably the world. The nave is built of oak logs split vertically in halves and set upright in a sill, also of oak. In 1960 dendro-magnetic tests suggested a date of about 835 for most of these nave timbers, although some were dated to an earlier building (mid-seventh century). The date of the tower, also of timber, is apparently uncertain, but part at least of the brick chancel is known to be early sixteenth century.

There is a painting, a small arched panel, of about 1500 of St Edmund in the church. This is most appropriate for tradition has it that the body of St Edmund rested here in 1013 on its journey to Bury St Edmunds from London, where the monks had taken it during a period of danger to prevent it from being stolen by the Danes. While fighting against their invading forces, Edmund, king of the East Angles, had himself fallen into the hands of the Danes. In 870, having rejected the enemy's terms and refused to renounce Christianity, he was tied to a tree, scourged with whips, shot to death with arrows, and finally beheaded. In the year 903 Edmund's body was enshrined at Bury St Edmunds and it was to this little Suffolk town that the monks were returning with the martyr's remains when they paused here, in Essex.

Over the years very few of the clergymen associated with Greensted church have sought or received publicity. One whose name has found its way into the history books was the Reverend Philip Ray who, towards the middle of last century, complained of meetings of the local branch of the Chartist Association being held on Sunday during the hours of divine service. The concern of the parson together with that of local farmers and magistrates caused great hostility to be directed at the members. The branch had, in fact, been started by five of the Tolpuddle Martyrs, three of whom attempted to start a new life by taking a seven-year lease of New House Farm, near Greensted, while two others settled on a farm at High Laver (the sixth soon returned to Tolpuddle in Dorset). The effect of the intense enmity they experienced in Essex drove the five martyrs to emigrate to Canada. It would appear that, in the opinion of certain of their contemporaries in the county, these agricultural labourers who had combined to resist wage reductions had not suffered enough. The Essex farmers of the time could not recognize the full pardon granted in 1836 following the martyrs' conviction on a trumped-up charge of administering illegal oaths and the sentence of seven years transportation, part of which they served in Botany Bay.

Next to Greensted church, in its somewhat isolated position,

is the hall. Mainly built towards the end of the seventeenth
century, its exterior is largely the result of work done in 1875.
Captain P. J. Budworth, who lived there, wrote a history of
Greensted and Ongar in 1876, revived the fair in Ongar, and
generally took such a keen interest in local affairs that the
Budworth Hall was built in Ongar as a memorial to him in
1886.

From Greensted one may travel by main roads, or thread
one's way across country along smaller roads, to Epping, a high
and pleasant residential centre to the north-east of Epping
Forest. As a roadside town on the old coach route from
London to Norwich, Epping had twenty-six inns as recently as
about 1800 and several still exist. Catering splendidly for
modern needs with its Epping Forest Motel is the Cock Inn.
The old inn attracted many interesting characters, among them
John Taylor, the 'water-poet', who ended up taking the
'Crown' public-house in Hanover Court, Long Acre. Born in
1580, he was apprenticed to a waterman, pressed for the navy,
and was present at the siege of Cadiz. Later, as a Thames
waterman, he increased his earnings by rhyming, travelling and
producing booklets with odd titles. On one occasion he started
from London to Queenborough in a brown-paper boat!
Narrowly escaping drowning, he lived to the age of 73.
Obviously no fool, he wrote:

Pens are most dangerous tools, more sharp by odds
Than swords, and cut more keen than whips or rods.

No doubt similar stories could be told about those who
frequented 'Epping Place' in High Road, Epping's principal inn
and posting house until well into last century. Now consisting
of two private houses – Winchelsea House and Epping Place,
the old inn is said to have been visited by O'Brien the Irish
giant (he is supposed to have been over eight feet tall) around
the end of the eighteenth century. There are tales of doors
being enlarged because of his height.

The dignified parish church of Epping, that of St John the
Baptist, was built in 1889, its noble tower, separated from nave
and aisle, being added twenty years later. The histories of other
buildings in the town are themselves commentaries on the

constantly changing political and social scene. Centrepoint Youth Centre was built in 1861 as a National school and within twenty-eight years 445 children were in attendance at a charge of twopence, less than one new penny, each a week. And a modern supermarket in High Street was originally built as a Town Hall, later being used as a cinema.

The mother church of Epping, originally a hamlet known as Epping Street, is at Epping Upland. Dedicated to All Saints, it is of twelfth-century origin, its buttressed and battlemented brick tower dating from the late sixteenth century. There is a brass to Thomas Palmer, Professor of Common Law at Cambridge who lived at the moated house, Gills, and died in 1621.

The A11 from Epping to London passes through Epping Forest and leading from it is the road to High Beach (sometimes spelt Beech), a pleasant and convenient place at which to complete our excursions from the county town. Holy Innocents, the Victorian grey stone church, is surrounded by trees among which its spire appears as a landmark for walkers. Over the years many people have delighted in the sights and sounds of this part of the forest. Tennyson, who lived at Beech Hill House (later called Beech Hill Park) from 1837 to 1840, wrote parts of *In Memoriam* here, including lines inspired by the sound of the bells of Waltham Abbey. He was going through a restless and unhappy period. His work had been ridiculed by critics and his friend Arthur Hallam had died at the age of twenty-two. Poor Tennyson did not see or hear the birds at High Beach and at first he found so much about the people "artificial, frozen, cold and lifeless". But his most bitter experience occurred when he lost his capital on the failure of the Patent Decorative Carving and Sculpture Company and the bankruptcy of its promoter, Dr Matthew Allen, proprietor of the private asylum at High Beach where John Clare, the "peasant poet", was a patient. "I have drunk", wrote Tennyson, "one of those most bitter draughts out of the cup of life, which go near to make men hate the world they move in."

Dr Allen may have been no businessman, but it must be made clear that he was something of a pioneer in the treatment of those affected by mental illness. Cultured, courteous, and humane, and well able to win the confidence, even the affection, of his patients, he had opened his asylum at High

Saffron Walden: an ancient corner

In Epping Forest

The Pier-end at Southend-on-Sea

White Street at Great Dunmow

Swans beside the River Stour at Mistley

Tower mill at Stansted Mountfitchet

Courtauld's factory at Halstead

New industrial estate at Halstead

Yardley factory at Basildon

New town skyline at Basildon

Beach in 1825. At a time when patients in public asylums were so often treated like 'cabbages', and embarrassing ones at that, Dr Allen arranged games and social visits for his patients, many of whom had their own keys and walked as they pleased in the forest.

Certainly John Clare's four years in Dr Allen's care brought him relief, if only temporarily. "The place here is beautiful", he told his wife, "the country is the finest I have ever seen." The good doctor, knowing only too well that the poet's return to his wife and seven children would bring relapse, set about securing a small annuity for him, but an appeal for five hundred pounds was unsuccessful. What a commentary on the shallow socialites who had once taken up John Clare for their own entertainment. Dr Allen remained loyal to his patient even after he left High Beach and walked the eighty miles to his old home at Northborough in Northamptonshire. "Whenever you like a little change", he wrote to Clare, "you are welcome to come here and get bed and board for nothing, and be at liberty to go and come as you choose . . ."

After this kind note, perhaps we should end this chapter with an extract from one of John Clare's poems of his Essex years:

> I love the Forest and its airy bounds,
> Where friendly Campbell takes his daily rounds:
> I love the breakneck hills, that headlong go,
> And leave me high, and half the world below;
> I love to see the Beech Hill mounting high,
> The brook without a bridge and nearly dry,
> There's Bucket's Hill, a place of furze and clouds,
> Which evening in a golden blaze enshrouds.

VI

THE NEW TOWNS

HARLOW on the western border of Essex, twenty-three miles north-east of London, and Basildon in the south-east of the county, twenty-nine miles from the capital, are two of eight new towns created under the New Towns Act 1946. Intended to relieve the congestion of London by removing people and industry beyond the Metropolitan Green Belt, they were planned as self-contained and balanced communities.

Harlow was designed by Harlow Development Corporation. Established in 1947, with full powers to acquire land, build houses, factories and shops, and provide all necessary services, this government-sponsored body invited Frederick (later Sir Frederick) Gibberd to prepare the master plan. This covered housing, industry, commerce, shops, schools, recreation, landscaping, and open space in the designated area, some 6,400 acres mainly taken from agriculture, and affecting about twenty-five smallholdings and larger farms. Originally about 4,500 people lived in the new town area, most of them in the north-east corner, in the village of Old Harlow. But within twenty-five years, with the development of the original master plan almost complete, the population had reached about 81,000, nearly 23,000 dwellings had been built, and some 130 firms operated in the town.

Harlow is built in neighbourhoods, each of about 5,000 people. The separation of these neighbourhoods from one another by green wedges of open space gives the town, as was originally intended, the appearance of having been grafted into the countryside rather than superimposed on it. Certainly Harlow, with nearly half its area still open and devoted to parks, playing fields, woodland and farmland for grazing animals, is a place where light, air and space are all abundant.

In the centre of each neighbourhood is a primary school and

next to this is a shopping centre and a meeting hall, a church and a public house. With main roads running outside the neighbourhood, it is possible for young children to walk to and from school much more safely than in most other towns. In addition to the little groups of shops in individual neighbourhoods, there are more shops in the neighbourhood centres, each serving a cluster of neighbourhoods, and in the town centre. Apart from shops, neighbourhood centres have other important features, including service industry areas, churches, libraries, community centres, and group medical, dental and clinic centres.

During the course of the comparatively short history of Harlow new town, there have been various changes not only in housing policy but in social and economic trends, and in building materials and techniques, while increased demands for garages and parking facilities have influenced the density of housing development. Added to all this is the fact that many different architects have been employed and the natural result is a wide variety of house design and of individual character in the neighbourhoods. Roughly four-fifths of homes in Harlow are two-storey houses. Most of the others are low-rise flats, though the nine high-rise blocks of flats are an important and striking feature of the town.

Now expanded as a neighbourhood of its own, the old village of Potter Street in the south-east sector of Harlow, where potters once plied their craft, includes new houses and flats and older properties too. Among the latter are the seventeenth-century White House Farm, the seventeenth- to eighteenth-century Kingsdon Hall, the eighteenth-century Baptist church, and four nineteenth-century buildings of special interest.

Old Harlow, in the north-east sector of the town, where the first of the new houses were built in 1949, has retained many of its old buildings. Harlowbury chapel, a Grade One building of outstanding national interest, is twelfth century. There are at least sixteen Grade Two buildings of special merit, while another nineteen on the supplementary list (Grade Three) include the fifteenth-century New Hall and two sixteenth-century buildings, the Crown Public House and the Churchgate Hotel.

During the course of the Old Harlow redevelopment scheme, subject of a Group A Civic Trust Award in 1971, the High Street, a thoroughfare fast becoming ruined by traffic chaos, was redeveloped as a traffic-free shopping precinct containing twenty-eight shops, a branch library and a bank. The design of the new buildings reflects the differing architectural character of the old ones, and, in accordance with local tradition, most of them have plaster walls painted a creamy-buff colour throughout.

Also in the north-east sector, the neighbourhood groups of Mark Hall (North and South) and Netteswell are early housing areas where a wide range of house types, mainly of traditional design, low-rise flats and four tower blocks have been built. Most of the homes in the neighbourhood groups of Brays Grove, Tye Green and Latton Bush, in the south-east sector of Harlow, were built by traditional methods to conventional designs during the last twenty years, though there are a few older properties in the old village of Tye Green and Commonside Road.

Non-traditional designs and building techniques have been widely used in the south-west cluster of neighbourhoods – Great Parndon, Passmores, Stewards, and Kingsmoor, the latest area to be built. Bishopsfield, the hilltop housing cluster in Passmores neighbourhood, has attracted considerable attention from architects and sociologists of many nationalities. Designed by Michael Neylan, as the result of an open housing competition, it makes use of a hillside site in a manner that is both original and skilful. In 'the Casbah', as this scheme is popularly known, flats and maisonettes are grouped on the higher part of the site around a central concrete podium (with garages below). Radiating from this down the hillside are patio bungalows with small but private gardens and narrow paved footways.

At The Maples in the Kingsmoor neighbourhood are Canadian-designed houses of timber construction, while at Milwards, in the same neighbourhood, are examples of the use of faced concrete blocks. Precast concrete slabs have been used at Clarkhill, and extruded asbestos panelling at Berecroft, both schemes in Stewards neighbourhood.

Preserved in the Great Parndon neighbourhood cluster are

eleven Grade Three buildings of special architectural and historic interest dating from the sixteenth and seventeenth to the nineteenth century. The eighteenth-century Passmores House in Third Avenue is classified as a building of special merit (Grade Two). A Georgian manor house with a few Victorian additions, it now houses Harlow Museum whose displays are devoted to local history, natural history, geology and folk life. The Friends of Harlow Museum Society, founded to support the museum as it developed, holds a regular weekly club night and arranges monthly lectures by guest speakers. Children's activities based on the museum include two Saturday clubs for girls and boys under twelve and a weekly club for those above that age. Schools visit the museum and day-time classes are organised there by the local Adult Education Centre. The museum courtyard houses some outside displays, while the grounds are public parkland where visitors may admire the fine trees, visit the butterfly garden, or follow a nature trail.

Passmores House is close to the Town Centre, an impressive and dominating mass of towers, office blocks and stores and one that contrasts well with the open countryside surrounding the town. Planned as a pedestrian shopping and entertainment centre, with surface and multi-storey car parks at its perimeter, The High, as the Town Centre is known, includes a 1,250-seat cinema, a bingo hall, the Playhouse theatre and arts centre, restaurants and snack bars, and some 200 shops. An open air market, gay with coloured awnings, is held on the Market Square, in the northern part of the Town Centre, three days a week and on Bank Holidays. At the south of the Town Centre is the cross-shaped Town Hall whose tower block, with its recessed top storeys and four-arched crown, dominates the scene. On the east the Town Hall is flanked by Crown offices, the police station, and an elegant courthouse. On its western side are St Paul's, the fine parish church built here in 1959, and Harlow Technical College, a group of one-, three-, and seven-storey buildings overlooking open country. In the middle of the southern edge of the Town Centre, the water gardens form a beautiful oasis, terraced gardens where water from a canal is discharged through lions' heads into another canal and then into lower pools.

There are two main industrial areas, covering some 300 acres. Temple Fields Industrial Area is by the railway, the London-Cambridge main line, in the north-east corner of Harlow, while Pinnacles Industrial Area lies on the western edge of the town. Linked to housing neighbourhoods and shopping centres by roads, independent cycle ways and pedestrian paths, the two main industrial areas were well separated from one another to avoid creating an 'east end' and a 'west end' to the town and to divide the traffic flow during peak hours.

Other industry is located in smaller estates associated with the neighbourhood shopping centres. These small industrial and service areas provide a certain amount of work for married women close to their homes. The industrial areas have been screened from residential areas by tree-planting, the creation of artificial mounds, and the use of landscape wedges.

West of Temple Fields Industrial Area and to the north of the Town Centre, the Town Park, 164 acres of rolling parkland set in a steeply wooded valley, stretches from Netteswell housing area to the Stort navigation canal. The intention has been to provide a wide variety of recreational, amenity and horticultural features in the park whose principal features include boating, cafe and car parks, children's assault course, dance floor, gardens, ice skating, paddling pool, pets corner, playgrounds, roller skating rink, show ground, specimen shrubbery, walled garden, and water gardens.

Spurriers, a Victorian mansion set in eight acres of grounds, is the focal point of much activity in the park. Camping by small groups of young people is encouraged, while the establishment of a pets corner in outbuildings behind the main building enables children to see and handle domestic animals that often cannot be kept in areas of high-density housing. The show ground near Spurriers is for the use of organisations wanting to put on major displays – fairs, circuses, rallies, and similar events.

On the other side of the park is the Road Safety Training Ground, a comparatively quiet area where young people may learn to cope with modern traffic conditions. It is realized that most people visiting the park will arrive by car and car parks have therefore been provided as natural entry points. All the same, roads are kept to a minimum, being bridged or tunnelled under wherever possible, and there are numerous access points for pedestrians and a cycle link connected with the town's independent network of cycle tracks.

The playgrounds in the Town Park were planned to provide for special occasions and to ensure variety, but they form a small part of the total area devoted to playgrounds in Harlow. It is, in fact, claimed that, in a town with over fifty such areas, few houses are more than a quarter of a mile from a children's playground.

The presence in the town of so many young people and children had naturally led to early demands for facilities for sports and outdoor recreation and, in 1958, the Development Corporation took the initiative leading to the formation of the Harlow and District Sports Trust. This body pioneered the town's finely equipped multi-purpose sports centre, a large and successful community project that caters for and is supported by people of all ages.

More than twenty-five indoor sports and games can be played in the large indoor sports hall where members can attend coaching courses and make use of the sauna bath, solarium, cafe, and licensed bars. Outdoor facilities include floodlit international standard running track, athletics area, all-weather training area, association football pitch, cricket and hockey ground, practice nets, grass practice area, ski-run, tennis courts, and children's playground. Open daily, the centre is used by over 100 clubs and has 7,000 individual members from seven years of age upwards.

Besides the outstanding facilities provided by the sports centre, there are many public sports grounds and a number of private ones. An eighteen-hole championship standard golf course designed by Henry Cotton lies in the valley of Canons Brook where an old farmhouse was adapted as a clubhouse and social centre. The Town Swimming-Pool, an indoor heated pool of championship standard, is a very popular feature of the Town Park, and the swimming-pools at several schools are also used by organizations in the evenings. The Stort provides opportunities for fishing and canoeing, and country lanes, integral features of the town, are safe for riding and cycling.

Harlow has played a keen and lively part in the revival and

development of the arts. In the early days, people, often in small groups, came together to make music and act in plays, and the new Methodist Church organized the first Eisteddfod. Then the Alberni String Quartet, Harlow's own group of resident professional musicians, was established by a grant from the Gulbenkian Foundation and is now supported by grants from the local authority and other bodies. Harlow Symphony Orchestra, Harlow Choral Society, and Harlow Youth Orchestra are among the local musical groups bringing credit to the town and making its name known well beyond the borders of Essex. What is so very pleasing is the enthusiasm of young people, many attending Saturday morning music schools and a number of whom have become members of the Essex Youth Orchestra and the National Youth Orchestra.

Hundreds of children have appeared in performances of 'Coppelia', the 'Nutcracker suite' and other ballets given by Harlow Ballet Club under the direction of Leo Kersley, leading male dancer of the Sadler's Wells Theatre Ballet (now Royal Ballet) from 1945-50. At least one ex-Harlow ballet student is now a professional dancer and several others have been accepted into the Royal Ballet School in London. Many other forms of dancing, including old-time, Scottish and folk dancing, are enjoyed in the town. Drama, too, has met with enthusiastic support in Harlow. The Moot House Players have performed here and abroad, the Netteswell Players have won the All-England Drama Finals, and other amateur groups are active.

The visual arts have also been encouraged and supported in Harlow. Pride of place must be given to the splendid work of the Harlow Art Trust, which, for more than twenty years, has been placing works of sculpture in the town until it now has nearly thirty, a larger collection than most big British cities. In his preface to *Sculpture in Harlow*, the fine illustrated catalogue of works acquired by the Trust, Henry Moore stressed that siting these works in the open brings them to the attention of many people who are not especially interested in art and enables sculpture to become a part of everyday existence.

Preference has been given to contemporary British sculpture, young sculptors being afforded opportunities for their work to be seen in permanent settings. There has been great interest in the more traditional works, even a strong affection for some of them, but the more abstract works are not always appreciated, some people questioning whether they can in fact be seriously regarded as works of art.

Henry Moore's *Family Group*, a work carved in Hadene stone, is sited in the Civic Square. This product of a great artist's individual creative genius belongs both to the past and the present, and the same is true of Moore's *Bronze Cross*, a tall bronze cast sited in the Water Gardens of the town centre. In the same gardens a bronze cast of Rodin's *Eve* makes a gentle but nevertheless strong impression. Carved in blue limestone, Barbara Hepworth's *Contrapuntal Forms* is beautifully sited in the Glebelands housing area. Originally commissioned for the 1951 South Bank Exhibition, it was afterwards chosen for Harlow in the distribution of the Festival of Britain works. Ralph Brown's powerful bronze, *Meat Porters*, is in the Market Square, Town Centre, near to F. E. McWilliam's *Portrait Figure*, a beautiful portrait of the sculptor Elisabeth Frink whose somewhat elegant *Boar* is in the Water Gardens. There are many more: I can only urge readers to go and see for themselves, to look not only in the open but in St Paul's church, in the Playhouse, outside the Central Library, and elsewhere.

There are several other organizations concerned with the visual arts: Harlow Society of Art, Harlow Photographic Society, and the Playhouse Co-operative Film Society – to mention but a few. This is all part of an amazing growth of voluntary organizations, clubs and societies, many concerned with leisure activities. Over the course of about thirty years some 500 clubs and societies have come into being, involving the use of nearly 150 common rooms, community centres, schools, church halls, and other premises.

Several thousands of members use the recreational and social facilities of the Community Associations. Based on community centres and common rooms in the neighbourhoods, these Associations are formed and run by the residents themselves with financial help from the County Council. They have attracted large numbers of voluntary workers, one having some 200 of these helpers. Attached to Community Associations (and some churches and other bodies) are Old Peoples' Clubs. These are well supported by retired people who have been praised for their ability to settle down quickly and to make their own distinctive contribution to the life of the town.

Community Associations also sponsor nursery play-groups. Later, at the beginning of the term before they reach their fifth birthday, children are admitted to neighbourhood infant schools. They transfer at seven years of age to junior schools, also sited in the neighbourhoods. Here they follow a four year course which is sufficiently wide and flexible as to include not only the more traditional academic subjects of the junior school but elementary science, music, French, and certain wider aspects of mathematics, too. Secondary education is provided at eight well-equipped comprehensive schools. Each serves its own area and is situated on the perimeter of the town or in one of the green wedges between neighbourhood clusters. Harlow is proud of its schools, all but one of which have been built since 1950, and its Technical College in the Town Centre where further and adult education are provided. There is satisfaction in the knowledge that pupils have left its schools for Oxford, Cambridge, London and other universities, for Colleges of Education and similar professional institutions. But this has not led the authorities to overlook the needs of handicapped children for whom Harlow's special schools and units provide an abundance of care and understanding.

These excellent qualities are also much in evidence in Harlow's concern for both the preventive and curative aspects of medical care. Helped by the Nuffield Provincial Hospitals Trust, the new town has developed a series of neighbourhood group practice and clinic centres, each part of an internationally recognised pioneer scheme in community health care. These health centres are places where patients' personal doctors may be consulted by appointment (as may dentists at most centres) and where regular clinics for mothers and babies are held. They are bases too for health visitors, district nurses and midwives, all of whom work in close co-operation with the doctors. Specialist centres, all built by the Nuffield Trust, house speech therapy, chiropody, physiotherapy and other clinics.

Industrial, office and shop workers are looked after by the Harlow Industrial Health Service, a non-profit making associ- ation staffed by industrial nursing sisters and the local doctors. With five centres, one on each of the two industrial estates and three others, this voluntary scheme is financed by employers. Besides providing medical and nursing treatment at its centres, the Industrial Health Service operates an emergency casualty service throughout the twenty-four hours of every day, advises on special hazards, runs first-aid courses in factories, and undertakes many other useful services.

In-patient care is provided in the hospital whose thirty-acre site is close to the Town Centre. Opened in 1965 by Princess Alexandra and named after her, this hospital is being developed in phases. The third of these has yet to be started, but its completion is expected to result in a complete district general hospital with more than 900 in-patient beds. The Princess Alexandra Hospital has maintained close and effective links with family doctors, health visitors, district nurses, midwives and other health service workers. Such co-operation is helping to make Harlow a healthy place in which to live.

Like that at Harlow, the new hospital at Basildon, the second of the new towns of Essex, will eventually have more than 900 beds. Opened in 1973, it was built in steps on a sloping site on the south side of the town. But, before discussing the development of Basildon in any further detail, it is important to recall that, in 1949 when the Development Corporation was appointed, some 4,500 of the 7,818 acres of its designated area included thousands of shacks and other substandard buildings, seventy-eight miles of unmade roads, and ill-planned shopping centres. These developments originated after the agricultural depression of the late nineteenth century. At that time many farms in the area were acquired by speculators who resold the land in small building plots to buyers who, all too often, were encouraged by the receipt of free rail tickets and the provision of free drink at the sale.

After the Second World War the local authorities concerned were unable to undertake the vast task of clearing what had become a large rural slum divided into some 30,000 ownerships. Accordingly they petitioned the minister to designate the area as the site of a New Town, and this action was taken early in 1949. The Development Corporation's outline plan suggested a population of 80,000 for Basildon New Town, including the 25,000 who already lived in the designated area. This figure was subsequently revised to 106,000, but the new Master

Plan envisages a population of 134,000 by the end of the century.

Now, with a population of 85,000, more than 20,000 homes, and some 200 factories, Basildon stretches for about six miles, from Pitsea in the east to Laindon in the west, the whole set around a new town centre. This is intended to be the commercial, administrative and recreational centre and to act as a focal point not only for the surrounding residential neighbourhoods but for the whole district. Planned as a pedestrian precinct, it is the site of the principal shops (more than 200), an open market, and parking facilities for some 4,000 cars. Maurice Lambert's *Mother and Child* here, in Town Square, symbolizes the young and growing area of Basildon whose District Council uses an interpretation of the statue as its symbol.

At the junction of the Town Square with East Square is Brooke House, a fourteen-storey block of eighty-four flats standing on eight twenty-seven-foot-high reinforced concrete 'pilotis' or V-shaped struts. This large structure, "a triumph of design" (as it has been described), makes a striking landmark and one that, being lived in, adds life to an area which might often otherwise be completely 'dead' in the evenings and at weekends. A more recent development at Basildon's town centre is Station House, a vast air-conditioned office building. Closely connected with the new station on the Fenchurch Street (London) – Southend line by a covered walkway, it should help to provide office jobs, the scarcity of which has led many workers to travel to London and Southend (it should also be remembered that many Ford employees and others travel in to Basildon to work).

At the geometric centre of the area, the town centre is a natural focal point not only for Basildon but also for the surrounding countryside, a situation creating its own pressures and problems. District Centres were proposed for Pitsea and Laindon. The first to be built was that at Laindon where a two-level circulation system, with the pedestrian shopping 'deck' above the roadway and service entries to shops, made effective use of a limited area. As 'overspill' centres, District Centres give some relief to the pressure on the Town Centre itself, as do the neighbourhood groups of nine to ten shops, small businesses satisfying many needs.

Originally nine residential neighbourhoods were planned, a tenth being added later, but the most recent Master Plan provides for twenty-seven by the end of the century. As in Harlow, the neighbourhoods have their own schools, shops, churches, public houses, open spaces, and other facilities. Many of their names (Laindon, Langdon Hills, Vange and Pitsea – to name a few) are traditional to the area.

In a *Times* Special Report, Patrick O'Leary urged that young town planners should hurry on down to Basildon. "There, more than in most new towns", he wrote, "they can study at first hand the rapid changes in housing and thinking that have taken place in twenty-five years." One can confirm just how right he was by moving across the town from east to west, the general direction in which building has proceeded. The first housing areas were developed east of the town centre in Barstable and Fryerns neighbourhoods. Here short terraces of brick-built houses, some white-rendered, were built at relatively low densities. Here, too, the open front gardens, roadside lawns, and trees, including many carefully preserved old ones, recall the Garden City pioneers whose personalities and ideas must have had striking influences on the planners of our new towns.

While agreeing that changes in the town's housing pattern owe something to new theories of urban form, Basildon Development Corporation have emphasized that the factors which really dictated change have been technological. The great increase in ownership and use of private cars in recent years has had particularly important effects. Once limited on government instructions to 15 for every 100 homes, garage and parking provision has become far more generous and realistic. The rear-access principle was gradually adopted as the new town grew, but it was at Lee Chapel North neighbourhood, north-west of the town centre, where separate vehicle and pedestrian routes were first developed throughout the entire neighbourhood.

In the later neighbourhoods one can also find abundant evidence of increases in housing density, the tendency towards an increasingly close-knit character. More space is often available within homes. Gardens may be smaller, but safe play areas are available. Changing methods in the building industry have made their mark, and houses built in Laindon and Vange neighbourhoods show signs of the break with traditional methods of house construction in favour of prefabrication. On many houses tiles and metal sheeting give the impression of real Essex weatherboarding. Similar concern for visual effects resulted in the unsightly confusion of overhead wires and aerials that spoils so many towns being avoided by the use of underground cables for telephones, radio and television.

During the early stages of its development, Basildon concentrated on the provision of family homes, mainly with three to four bedrooms, to satisfy the needs of the largest element of the community, young married couples with small children. Later the arrival of elderly parents and young unmarried workers brought about changes in the population structure and the need for more small dwellings. Groups of old people's maisonettes and bungalows with resident wardens and communal meeting rooms have been built, and clubs, meals on wheels, and other welfare services are available.

When the original plan for the establishment of the new town of Basildon was prepared it was recognized that healthy growth depended very largely on the development of housing and industry being suitably balanced. At first industry was not easily attracted, one serious disadvantage being that the area was not commercially developed. Nowadays more people realise that the Thames is only a few miles to the south, the City of London is only thirty-six minutes by rail from the new town centre railway station, Tilbury Dock, Dartford Tunnel and Southend Airport are not far away, and Europe is close.

It was the arrival in Basildon of a few internationally-known firms that initiated real industrial growth and prosperity. Factories now range in size from small workshops and nursery factories to the Ford Tractor Plant with $1\frac{1}{4}$ million square feet of workspace on a 100-acre site. This industry is sited on the north side of the town, alongside the Southend arterial road but separated from it by stretches of grass and trees. The Ford Tractor Plant, a notable factory by E. R. Collister and Associates, incorporates an important landmark, a huge water tower consisting of a large sphere balanced on a slender tubular shaft. The Yardley factory by John D. Morgan and David C. Branch, a beautiful building on a nineteen-acre site, is one of the most modern and well-planned cosmetics factories in the world. There are, of course, points of interest in many other industrial and commercial buildings in the town.

People seeking refresher courses or new skills many undergo training at the government-sponsored skill centre, one of fifty-five such places in Britain. The College of Further Education, situated at Nethermayne, has departments of general education, engineering and business studies. Primary and secondary schools are situated within reasonable distances of all homes in the town and, in addition, play-groups for the very young are run in all neighbourhoods, usually in local community halls.

Like their colleagues in other parts of the country, teachers and youth leaders in Basildon must, at least occasionally, introduce games and other forms of recreation to their pupils and club members who later find them developing into absorbing leisure pursuits. This is vital work because, since the original master plans for Basildon and the other new towns were produced, the pattern of leisure has changed. This has created opportunities for many more people to take part in a widening range of spare-time activities, and considerable efforts have been made in Basildon to provide facilities for them.

In 1968 Lord Goodman, Chairman of the Arts Council of Great Britain, opened the Arts Centre, a temporary building which it is hoped to replace by permanent accommodation in the proposed new civic centre. Situated in the town centre, it has a theatre seating 454, studios for pottery, painting, music and photography, a comfortable lounge bar, and exhibitions of the work of local and other artists. The local council, Basildon and District Arts Association, and independent groups use the theatre to bring many forms of entertainment to the town, opera, jazz, classical music, ballet, poetry and pantomime having all been presented there. Not the least important are amateur productions by drama groups and other local societies. Films are shown at the Arts Centre and also at two cinemas opened in 1971 in the town centre.

Excellent facilities for sport and outdoor recreational activity are available in Basildon whose Sports Council encourages, develops and co-ordinates all forms of sport in the district.

There are clubs for all forms of indoor sport. Among them is Kingswood Squash Club at Sparrows Herne. Overlooking the golf course, its modern premises include ten international standard air-conditioned courts, a bar and lounges, and a 'squashshop'. Squash is also played at Aquatels, the large family recreation centre next to Ford's Tractor Plant on the industrial estate. Originating as the idea of a local businessman, Mr R. Treble, this recreation centre covers 105 acres and includes a public house, a country club, a golf-driving range, a ski school, riding stables and a fishing lake.

Basildon Bowl, the ten-pin bowling alley in the town centre, had closed, but the council decided to lease part and it now operates ten of the twenty-four lanes, the rest of the place being used for bingo. The covered and heated swimming-pool in the southern part of Gloucester Park, close to the town centre, is well used. With a main championship-size pool and a teaching-pool, it is open to the public throughout the week, private and class instruction being provided on weekday evenings.

Gloucester Park, the 355-acre town park, lies in the north-west quarter of the town. The six-acre fishing lake, north of the swimming-pool, is a central feature. On the town centre side there are pitches for football, rugby football and cricket, and other facilities, including an artificially-surfaced practice cricket wicket, a floodlit hard-surfaced play area, a floodlit running-track and a field events area. A café and bar administered by the Basildon Sports Council Club are situated in the Murrayfield Pavilion where there is changing accommodation with showers too.

Many young people are among those who play golf on the council's eighteen-hole par seventy course, a well-used and attractive amenity off Sparrows Herne in the southern part of the town. Basildon Golf Club provides club facilities at the course where on occasion keen young players may be seen going round after finishing nightshift in a factory.

Besides the recreational areas already mentioned, there are at least seventeen play areas, recreation grounds and other open spaces, ranging in size from 2 to 17.8 acres, some with children's playground equipment, others with a variety of pitches, tennis courts, and bowling-greens.

At Pitsea, the 100-acre Sea Transport Depot is being developed for dinghy sailing, camping and adventure. These activities are in complete contrast to many of the facilities provided within the town, certain of which strike some people as being either too sophisticated or too organized. The Development Corporation have long sympathized with such feelings. They have also recognized the need for open spaces for casual recreation, casual walking and sitting, perhaps, as they have called it, "the most important but least provided for adult activity".

Basildon residents (and others) who are interested in quiet rambles or just sitting are fortunate in that, during the inter-war years, Essex County Council, with inspired foresight, acquired attractive open spaces at Westley Heights, One Tree Hill and Langdon Hills, all in, or close to, the south-west area of the new town. These linked areas of woodland and common include some of the highest land in Essex, affording fine views of the surrounding countryside and of the lower reaches of the Thames.

Langdon Hills East (130 acres) and Langdon Hills West (133.75 acres), both administered by Essex County Council, are listed as Country Parks by the Countryside Commission. In the Langdon Hills, to the north of the road Staneway, a forty-acre nature reserve will be opened in 1978. Planned by Basildon Development Corporation, Basildon Council, Basildon Natural History Society, and the Nature Conservancy Council, it will be looked after by the Natural History Society with help from Basildon Development Corporation. It is hoped that the public will be able to walk through the reserve along a defined route, which will be developed into a nature trail. The Development Corporation believe that the nature reserve will form both a useful educational facility and a valuable amenity for the people of Basildon. For the interesting plants, including wild service trees and spotted orchids, and the badgers and other animals, it will, with proper management and the co-operation of local people, be an effective wild life sanctuary in an area where town and country meet and intermingle.

It is in Langdon Hills, half-way down Old Church Hill, that the small church of All Saints stands, its brick nave and chancel dating from the early sixteenth century; it has been turned into a private residence. On the hill above is the church of St Mary the Virgin. Built in 1876, this tall and narrow, somewhat grim building in its romantic woodland setting is a reminder of Victorian times when the Basildon area was still a region of small communities. Holy Cross Church in Church Road marks the centre of the old village of Basildon. Close to schools and a recreation ground bearing its name, and not far from the industrial area and Fryerns shopping centre, it bears a weather-vane dated 1702, a comparatively recent feature of a small church whose fourteenth-century nave and chancel were rebuilt in brick in 1597.

One mile north-west of the town centre, St Nicholas, Laindon, crowns a steep and wooded eminence. Its black weatherboarded belfry with crowning broach-spire forms an historical landmark, while the Purbeck type font provides continuity from the thirteenth-century to the present day. Basildon and Laindon children were educated in the seventeenth-century Priest's House, a timbered annexe at the west end of the church, until late in the nineteenth-century.

All Saints, Vange, its nave including the remains of a Norman window, and St Michael's, Pitsea, whose sixteenth-century tower was considerably restored during the rebuilding of 1871, are on high ground on Basildon's southern boundary, the latter occupying a magnificent viewpoint, a situation often considered to be one of the finest of any English church. In Church Road off Lower Dunton Road, St Mary's, Dunton, a church rebuilt in 1873, retains its sixteenth-century cup and paten, while in Nevendon Road, south of the A.127 road near one of Basildon's industrial estates, the small church of St Peter embodies parts dating from the fourteenth and fifteenth, and possibly the thirteenth, centuries. New churches have appeared as the New Town developed, St Chad, Vange, and St Basil the Great, Barstable, being fine examples. But many years will pass before they acquire the atmosphere of the ancient buildings.

There are still some very old houses in Basildon. Pitsea Hall, a timber-framed and plastered house of about 1600, is near the level crossing at Pitsea Railway Station, and Great Chalvedon Hall, a tall sixteenth-century timber-framed and weatherboarded manor house, is in Rectory Road, Pitsea. There are some nice old houses near the church at Nevendon, too.

Frampton's Farm, a T-shaped sixteenth-century building, and Nevendon Hall, its red brick dating from about 1800, are the most noteworthy.

These and other old buildings must surely have been admired by Reginald Beckett, the now forgotten author of *Romantic Essex*, who, in 1901, urged his readers to go into "undiscovered" Essex and there find fresh beauties for themselves. How surprised he would be if he could but return to seek the "very primitive" people in the lonely hills near Laindon, those who looked at him with open-eyed wonder, "almost as at a being from another world". And what would he make of modern Harlow? "A mile of unavoidable high road, terminating in a hill," he wrote, "brought me to Harlow. No sooner had I passed the first two or three houses than the town ended, and there were the green fields beyond. I rubbed my eyes, and thought that Harlow must be further on." Now, in the late 1970s, smiling at Beckett's impressions, we may doubt whether his "romantic Essex" still exists. But we could do far worse than to start our search in either of the county's two twentieth-century new towns, for their creation has not been entirely lacking in the visionary elements of romance.

VII

THE GOOD EARTH

"Most fatt, frutefull, and full of profitable things exceding (as farr as I can finde) anie other shire, for the general comodeties, and the plentie . . . this shire seemeth to me to deserve this title of the englishe Goshen, the fattest of the Lande; comparable to Palestina, that flowed with milke and hunnye." That was how Essex was described in 1594 by John Norden, the topographer who appears to have been particularly well impressed by the size and thickness of cheeses made in Rochford Hundred.

The soil of Essex continues to be highly productive but many marked changes have occurred since Norden's time and are indeed still taking place. One is the great demand from housing, industrial and other interests for land whose loss to agriculture amounts to some 500 acres a year. Another is mechanization whose development in arable farming has resulted in the use of large capacity tractors and large implements. Their efficient use has often involved the enlargement of fields and in many cases of farms themselves. The consequences of such changes have included the removal of hedgerows, copses and spinneys, and the reduction of regular labour at the rate of about 4 to 5 per cent a year.

According to *Agricultural Statistics England and Wales 1973*, a publication of the Government Statistical Service, there were 647,398 acres under crops and grass in Essex, a county whose total area (excluding water) was given as 903,828 acres. Forty-one per cent of the county's 4,316 agricultural holdings were under twenty acres and accounted for less than 2 per cent of the land. Only 56 of the 2,537 holdings of twenty acres and over extended to 1,000 acres or more, holdings of 300 to 499¾ acres being more numerous than those of any other size. Just over half of the farms in Essex are owner-occupied. Many of them are 'family' enterprises, as is also the case with rented

116

properties. The influence of London is just one factor responsible for the 'urban', rather than 'rural', outlook of a large
number of these farming families.

Much of the county's agricultural land is regularly ploughed,
cereals, notably wheat and barley, being major crops in an area
where yields and quality are often high. But there has been a
swing, at the expense of ploughing, to a minimal cultivation
technique prior to sowing cereals, and even about 2 per cent of
winter wheat is now direct-drilled without any cultivations at
all. Essex, where more than 209,000 acres were devoted to this
crop in 1973, grows the largest acreage of wheat in the country.
Many farmers grow two successive crops of winter wheat,
frequently trying a third. Apart from comparatively small
amounts sold for seed and for industrial purposes, Essex-grown
wheat is used for human food and livestock feed. Much of that
forming part of the human diet is blended with strong wheat
(mostly from Canada) and milled to form a mixed grist for
bread-making. Another important fraction is used for biscuits,
the remainder for household flour, commercially-produced
cakes, sausages, pie casings, rusks, pet foods, brewing adjuncts
and other miscellaneous uses.

Official estimates give an average yield of 34.1 hundred
weight of wheat per acre in Essex (1968-72), the comparable
figure for England and Wales being 32.4. But in 1974 a
competition organised by the National Seed Development
Organization, the marketing agency for the official plant
breeding stations of the United Kingdom, produced some
much higher yields from crops of Maris Huntsman, the first
British winter wheat to be added to the French official list of
varieties. Some ninety farmers produced yields of 60 hundred
weight and more per acre. The winning verified yield, amount-
ing to 86.1 hundredweight per acre, came from a farm in
neighbouring Suffolk, but Essex farmers also did well in the
competition. For example, a crop grown on medium clay on a
616-acre mixed farm at Felsted produced 72.03 hundred
weight per acre over 7.25 acres. Such outstanding yields resulted from a harvest that followed a good growing season, but
one must not overlook the dedication and attention to details
of the farmers or the high qualities of the wheat variety
concerned. Nowadays most Essex wheat is cut and threshed by

combine harvesters and these machines, first introduced to Britain in 1928, are a familiar sight on farms. But visitors to the county may occasionally find wheat being threshed in the old manner, by drum, to provide straw for thatching, combined straw being unsuitable for this purpose.

Barley is the second most important cereal grown in Essex, but, unlike wheat which has increased, its acreage has declined, The grain of this cereal with awned spikes, whose domestication, like that of wheat, occurred long ago, is a vital raw material to meat producers and maltsters. Although some is fed to livestock on farms where it is grown, quantities of barley are sold to other farmers who specialize in rearing and fattening cattle and pigs whose conversion of grain into meat provides protein-rich food for human consumption. Some higher-grade barley is sold to maltsters whose trade was formerly undertaken in several parts of the county but is now concentrated at Mistley, Witham, and one or two other places. The malt products themselves are sold to the brewing, bakery and food manufacturing industries, and there is a growing demand from home brewers. Barley straw, like that from other cereal crops, has all too often been burnt in recent years, but during the harvest of 1975 farmers from Wales and the West Country were only too pleased to buy it in Essex for use as fodder on their drought-stricken farms.

Oats are grown in Essex, as is a very small amount of rye. But these crops attract far less attention than maize, a taller and bulkier plant and one that still seems to lend a somewhat exotic touch to our countryside. The fact that maize has come to be recognized as a substitute for and supplement to grass silage and feeding barley has led to a dramatic rise in the acreage of both grain and silage maize in recent years. Maize is grown for three purposes – grain, silage, and zero grazing – in Britain where its acreage has risen from 1,000 to 50,000 acres since 1967. The area of maize is still comparatively small in Essex where by far the largest amount is grown for silage, but it is interesting to recall that valuable pioneering work in maize was carried out in the county by Hurst, the Witham-based wholesale seedsmen, seed breeders and growers. In the 1950s, when maize was almost unknown in Britain, they started research into the adaptability of North American and Continental inbreds for the British climate. This led to a large hybrid maize breeding programme and the successful introduction of the first British-bred maize varieties, Kelvedon 33 and 59A, names commemorating the little Essex town where they were bred. Sweet corn, a crop that is quite distinct from maize (in which it arose as a natural mutant), is the subject of a separate Hurst breeding programme. The Kelvedon area is an important centre for the production of small seeds (flower and other small seeds) and, of course, grass seed production is carried on throughout the county.

Potatoes, beans for stockfeeding, and sugar beet are other important Essex farm crops. In many places cultivation of the last-named crop no longer involves the large numbers of casual workers formerly engaged on sugar beet singling early in the growing season. For modern farming methods with their chemical sprays, monogerm seed and precision drills, have made it possible for much of the sugar beet acreage to be drilled and not touched again until it is harvested. After harvesting, now largely a mechanized operation, Essex-grown beet is sent to the sugar beet factory at Felsted or to that at Ipswich, where sugar is extracted.

There is not sufficient space to mention all the other agricultural crops of Essex, but the great value of grasses, as constituents of both permanent grass and rotation grasses, cannot be overlooked. Grazed or cut for silage or hay, they are important foods for livestock, contributing greatly to the production of milk and meat. Lucerne (or alfalfa), a long-rooted, drought-resisting fodder-plant, covers some 4,000 acres in Essex. As is the case with the clovers, those useful pasture plants, and other *Leguminosae*, the nitrogen-fixing bacteria in its root nodules convert the nitrogen of the atmosphere into nitrogenous plant food.

The same is true of the agricultural lupins being investigated by the Hurst organisation in Essex. One of them, *Lupinus albus*, has begun to show great promise, particularly two varieties from the Ukranian Research Institute for Agricultural Technology. This development is of considerable interest because the sweet white seeds of several new Australian varieties of another lupin species yield a nutritious meal suitable for feeding to pigs and poultry, and there is talk of their use as the source of a textured vegetable product similar to soya-bean extract. Grown here on occasion as green manure on light soils, lupins may now be bred not only for their seeds but also for use as animal food in the form of silage.

Many Essex farmers do not need this and other types of fodder because they do not keep livestock. But those who, over the years, have bred and reared farm animals have shown considerable interest in food matters and other developments, making, for example, sterling contributions towards building up the national dairy herd and in helping to strengthen individual breeds.

The history of the British Friesian, the popular and ubiquitous black and white dairy breed, is a case in point. The prefix Terling occurs frequently in the pedigrees of individuals of this breed, recalling the vital work of Edward Strutt of Terling, breeder of dairy cattle, pioneer of modern milk production, and, in the opinion of many of his contemporaries, the greatest agriculturist in the England of his day. In 1882, at the age of twenty-eight, the Hon. Edward Gerald Strutt, fifth son of the second Lord Rayleigh, had assumed the management of the Essex estate of his brother, the third Lord Rayleigh, the eminent mathematician and physicist and winner of the Nobel Prize for Physics. The times were hard, but energy, efficiency and the application of business principles helped him to extend Lord Rayleigh's farms to some 17,000 acres, to lay the foundations of the group of famous Friesian herds, and to start supplying London with fresh, safe milk through the medium of clean, well-equipped shops – Lord Rayleigh's Dairies, as they became known.

Strutt's efforts and example undoubtedly encouraged many other farmers to work and struggle through a long farming depression. Since then various sections of agriculture have suffered periodical setbacks, but the proximity of London has continued to influence the development of dairy farms, with a trend towards larger herds, and the Friesian continues to be regarded as "the world's cow". Friesians bred on Essex farms have been exported to many parts of the world. Recently, for example, the Iraqi Ministry of Agriculture purchased eleven heifers from Roydon Hall Farm, Ramsey, near Harwich, whose herd had previously produced animals for export to Abu Dhabi and Rumania.

In Britain itself, Essex Friesians have won many coveted awards. The Shopland herd of pedigree and accredited British Friesians, founded in 1922 at Temple Farm, Prittlewell, Southend-on-Sea, has been particularly successful. Shopland Lady Seabreeze RML created a record as the first cow to give eight consecutive 2,000 gallon lactations, bringing to the attention of people throughout the world not only its own outstanding yield but also the name of Shopland, the Essex parish whose separate identity virtually ceased with the demolition of its Norman church in the late 1950s. Shopland cows have won the female championship at the Royal Show in three out of the last eight years, and there is every indication that the herd will continue to uphold its high reputation.

The Ayrshire, Guernsey and Jersey – all dairy breeds, and the Hereford, a beef breed, are also seen in Essex. The latter is still popular for crossing in the dairy herd. The use of a Hereford bull on a Friesian cow ensures the continuance of the milk flow and produces a calf whose parentage is revealed by a combination of the characteristic black skin of the dam and the white face of the sire. This cross-bred calf, having somewhat thicker flesh than the pure dairy breed, is usually reared for beef. At Great Holland, a 3½-year old Hereford–Friesian cross-bred cow, that had been retained for breeding, distinguished itself by giving birth to triplets, two heifers and a bull, just one year and eighteen days after producing twins.

Certain Essex farmers have earned praise for their work as pioneers in importing and developing foreign and lesser-known breeds. Early in the 1960s, the county, where this breed was exhibited during the Royal Show at Chelmsford in 1856, received some of the early introductions of Charolais, excellent beef animals that are numerically the second largest breed of cattle in France. With a quiet disposition, these large white cattle are efficient grazers whose growth-rate is impressive. Nowadays the Essex Show has classes for Charolais which must be of full French origin or have passed inspection for entry into the British Pedigree Register. The bulls are in great demand for crossing with dairy cows, the cross-bred calves growing faster, with a better food conversion rate than crosses by British beef breeds, and having more lean meat and much less fat.

Simmental cattle are also kept in Essex and exhibited at the County Show. Originating as dual-purpose animals in Switzerland, they are now found throughout Europe and in the U.S.A. Simmentals are hardy and thrifty, and, like Charolais, have their own breed society in Britain. The import from France of the Limousin, a pure beef breed, was authorised as recently as 1970 and this, too, has appeared in Essex. A sturdy, dark brown animal, it is noted for rapid growth and high liveweight gains. The improvement of this ancient breed has taken place largely during the last one hundred years, especially since 1886 when the Limousin herd book was established, and it will be interesting to watch its development here and in other parts of Britain. Again in recent years, Essex cattle breeders have taken up the Australian Murray Grey breed, and already three young bulls, Great Bentley Star, Great Bentley Greg, and Tendring Jon, have brought into prominence at the Royal Show the names of the Essex villages where they were born.

For many years the name of the county itself was borne by the Essex Saddleback, a black pig with a white shoulder belt whose name was sometimes shortened to the Essex. Although the first Herd Book dates from 1919, the breed had been known locally in Essex for many years before then. In 1968 the Essex and Wessex Saddleback breeds were merged to form the British Saddleback, a dual-purpose breed for the production of both pork and bacon. During the Georgian period, when large numbers of pigs were bred and fattened in Essex for the London market, Charles Callis Western (the first and only Baron Western), politician and agriculturist of Felix Hall, Kelvedon, boasted of the qualities of the 'Essex Half Black' and advocated the use of hogs to convert corn into cash.

Since that time other breeds have been introduced into the county and at the June census of livestock on agricultural holdings in 1973 there were some 287,000 pigs in Essex, including 31,000 sows for breeding and 1,400 boars being used for service. Many of these animals are kept in pig units forming part of the farming system on large arable farms.

The Essex Show featured classes for Essex, Large Black, Large White and Middle White pigs in 1948. The prize list for 1976 includes classes for Large White, Welsh, and commercial pigs (pure breed or cross-bred). Saddlebacks are still kept as a breed and they are crossed with Large White pigs to produce cross-breds, which are often considered to have a lower incidence of infant mortality and also the ability to utilize their food more efficiently than the purebreds.

In the 1950s the Landrace was introduced from Sweden and this breed has since played a vital part in the pig industry not only in Essex but in Britain as a whole. Descended from the indigenous white pig of Scandinavia and Eastern Europe, the breed had been improved by selection based on progeny-testing. With a long body and other appropriate qualities, it had been developed for bacon production, and it was not long before Essex-bred Landrace were taking prizes in bacon classes at important shows.

Landrace and Large White boars are supplied by Elite Hybrids Ltd, the Colchester-based firm which is officially designated a Pig Breeding Company in the Meat and Livestock Commission's National Pig Improvement Scheme. This company's policy is designed to give commercial breeders the advantage of fully hybrid female parents and pure-line perform-ance-tested males for the maximum economic production of quality pig meat over a wide range of slaughter weights. Elite Hybrids have sold stock to breeders in Britain and many other parts of the world, and for several consecutive years one of the four herds forming their nucleus stock (that at Weeley Heath, near Colchester) has won the Dunmow Flitch Bacon Company's award for the highest percentage of A1 carcases sent to their factory at Dunmow under contract.

At the June 1973 census, the number of sheep in Essex amounted to some 49,000, about half of this population being under one year old. Compared with counties like Cornwall (407,000), Devon (1,329,000), and Durham (347,000) – to take but three examples from the beginning of the list – the Essex figure is not large. Sheep may be seen in comparatively small flocks on about 300 Essex farms where they often prove to be useful scavengers on herbage seed crops and economical in their own right when kept under conditions that are more intensive than the average.

In its early years the Essex Agricultural Society's annual Essex County Show included classes for 'long wool' and 'short wool' sheep. By 1948 it was catering for Suffolk sheep only and nowadays sheep are not represented there. The Suffolk breed is still seen in the county. Short-woolled, dark-faced and hornless, it is one of the 'Down' breeds. Another of these, the Hampshire Down, with its deep rich brownish black face and legs, is bred in Essex. But many sheep seen in the county are cross-bred, animals often developing the so-called hybrid vigour, whose possession gives greater resilience than either parent to environmental conditions, and conforming to the butcher's demand for good quality, quick-maturing lambs. Cross-bred animals are themselves used for breeding for fat lamb production as, for example, when mule ewes, the result of crossing a Border or Hexham Leicester with a Scottish Blackface or Swaledale ewe, are put to a Suffolk ram.

Turning to poultry, we find that the number of birds on agricultural holdings in Essex (more than four millions in 1973) is large compared with the figures for many other counties. Roughly 75 per cent of Essex poultry are officially classed as fowls (what the layman calls chickens), the remainder being made up of ducks, geese and turkeys. More than half the fowls are kept for the production of eggs, the majority for eating, the others for hatching. While there are many small producers, who often advertise their free-range eggs at the roadside, about half the eggs are produced by a relatively few large specialists whose birds are managed under mechanized battery systems or in deep litter units. The remaining fowls are reared for the table, the majority as broilers by relatively few large organizations. The insulated, mechanically ventilated broiler houses are now a familiar sight in parts of the countryside, anathema to those who hanker for the sight of fowls scratching on the farmyard dunghill, but a sure way of producing small chickens quickly and economically.

Ducks and geese account for only a small fraction of the number of poultry on agricultural holdings in Essex, but the position of turkeys is stronger. There were about 4,000 turkey hens for breeding in the county in 1973 (a small number when compared with the 86,000 in Norfolk) and some 88,000 other turkeys (including stags). Most of these birds are, in the modern manner, reared under intensive conditions, a far cry from the days when turkeys roosted in trees and large flocks were driven along the roads to London as Christmas approached.

One attractive event of the country year has survived to delight resident and visitor alike, namely blossomtime in the orchards. Orchard fruit is an important feature of Essex farming, being concentrated around the Colchester area but stretching as far south as Chelmsford. The area of orchards grown commercially has declined. Even so, Essex, with 7,700 acres, had the fourth largest acreage of such orchards in England and Wales in 1973, being overtaken only by Kent, Worcestershire and Herefordshire – in that order.

A most important orchard fruit here, Cox's Orange Pippin, an apple with good keeping qualities, gained its great popularity largely as the result of its magnificent flavour. Less popular, though still grown, is the county's own apple, the D'Arcy Spice, whose synonyms include Baddow Pippin, Essex Spice, and Pepin de Baddow. Now included in the National Fruit Trials collection, it originated in 1785 or earlier in the garden of the hall at Tolleshunt D'Arcy, and was introduced as a variety for cultivation in 1848 by John Harris, a nurseryman of Broomfield (or Baddow) as the Baddow Pippin. With firm, crisp flesh and a rich sweet flavour, it serves as a dessert apple for February and March, but unfortunately its somewhat rough and tough skin is considered to be a serious defect.

One important grower of orchard fruits (and small fruits also) is the family firm of Wilkin and Sons Limited of Tiptree, owners of a freehold estate of about 1,000 acres, whose five farms are at Tiptree (three), Tollesbury and Goldhanger. Cherries, greengages, plums, quinces, damsons, crab apples, apples, and medlars are all grown on their farms for use in jams and jellies which carry the name of Tiptree, Essex, to America, Germany, France, Canada, and nearly thirty other countries, including Afghanistan, Australia, Brazil, Japan and Iceland. Wilkins are convinced that part of the success which they have achieved in a business that employs about 200 people regularly and many more on a seasonal basis, and produces more than 2,000 tons of preserves a year, has been due to the quality of the fruit and also to the fact that only entirely natural materials are used.

Arthur Charles Wilkin, founder of the firm, settled at

Trewlands Farm, Tiptree, in 1859, began fruit farming there five years later, and started making jam in an old corn barn in 1885. Soon after his death in 1913, Tiptree Hall Farm, adjacent to Trewlands Farm, was purchased. This had earlier been the scene of John Joseph Mechi's energetic and enthusiastic fight for better farming, becoming by the 1850s what one eminent agricultural expert said was "in effect, a National Experimental Farm on which new implements, new theories, and new ideas were tried out."

Mechi, London-born son of an Italian refugee, made a lot of money from sales of his 'magic razor strops' and patent lamp for the illumination of shop window fronts before turning his attention to farming and the countryside. He provided Tiptree with a church and a school, founded the Royal Agricultural Benevolent Institution, and became an Alderman of the City of London, Sheriff of Middlesex, and one of the five members of the Board of the Royal Agricultural College at Cirencester. In 1857 his book *How to Farm Profitably* was published and 420 of his friends had presented him with a fine piece of silverwork, 3 feet 6 inches high, weighing 500 ounces, and costing between £500 and £600, in token of their appreciation of his continuous efforts to promote the interests of agriculture. Sadly, Mechi went on to suffer heavy losses in connection with his business interests and then Tiptree Hall fell on evil times – a famine winter for stock, two droughty summers, rinderpest, wet summers and disastrous harvests all taking their toll. In 1880, a few days before Christmas, he died a poor man but one recognized for the integrity of his personal character.

Ten years after Mechi's death Walter (later Sir Walter) Gilbey formed the Elsenham Jam Company whose successor is Elsenham Quality Foods Limited. Gilbey, who founded the well-known firm of wine merchants, had made his home at Elsenham Hall in north-west Essex. One of his great delights was to have preserves made for distribution as gifts for his friends. Made according to old recipes of the countryside from fruit grown locally (some in his own garden), Gilbey's jams were very well received, and so, at a time of agricultural depression, he went into production commercially, employing the men of his estate. Jam-making continued after his death. Then, in 1959, the present chairman, Mr A. J. G. Blunt, a fruit farmer himself, took over the company, then employing six people and running at a loss. The decision was made to return to the original high quality recipes and, even though the product was then advertised as the most expensive jam in the world, the business expanded considerably and many more people, all from local villages, are employed. A few years ago the firm started exporting its products, now including liqueur conserves, sauces and the famous gentlemen's relish Patum Peperium, and exports now account for about 20 per cent of its turnover. Thus the name of another Essex village is carried all over the world on jars of preserves made from damsons, greengages, Victoria plums and other fruits grown in the county.

The names of Tiptree and Elsenham also appear on jars of preserves made from such Essex-grown small fruit as strawberries, blackcurrants, gooseberries, loganberries and red currants. The list of acreages devoted to small fruit in the counties of England and Wales shows Essex lying sixth with 1,725 acres. The greater part of this area is devoted to blackcurrants, mostly for processing, and strawberries.

Considering the area of land devoted to the production of vegetables (excluding potatoes) for human consumption in the county, Essex is placed sixth among the counties of England and Wales. Some 15,000 acres, equivalent to more than half the land used for vegetables in the county, is given over to peas, the major part to peas for harvesting dry, another large acreage to green peas for canning, quick freezing and dehydration, and a smaller area to green peas for market. French beans for processing account for another large acreage, as do cabbages. Among the many other vegetables grown in Essex are Brussels sprouts, savoys, winter greens, cauliflowers, beetroot, parsnips, broad beans, runner beans, lettuce and onions.

Glasshouses, the majority heated, occupy some 400 acres in Essex. Many are situated near the coast and in the Lea Valley which, straddling the Essex-Hertfordshire border, produces the bulk of English cucumbers, a large proportion of tomatoes, and such other crops as carnations, roses and chrysanthemums. The acreage under glass continues to decline in the Lea Valley, and part of the industry is moving to the Clacton area where the light is good.

Roses, just mentioned, brought fame to Essex long ago, and today plants are exported from the county to Canada, Jamaica, America, Dubai, and other parts of the world. Cants of Colchester are the oldest rose growers in Britain, having been established in 1765, and among the foremost rose specialists of the world. Visitors to the rose fields between late June and the end of September may see for themselves the large number of colourful varieties grown.

In recent years, Cant's new rose successes have included Just Joey, a Hybrid Tea bush rose raised by the firm and awarded the Royal National Rose Society Trial Ground Certificate. A hardy plant of branching habit, it bears large scented blooms of coppery orange veined red, paling slightly to the frilled edges of the petals. Alpine Sunset, another successful Hybrid Tea bush rose raised by Cants and awarded the R.N.R.S. Trial Ground Certificate, has large fragrant blooms of creamy yellow flushed peach pink. Cants have, of course, bred many other beautiful roses and, deservedly, in 1974 they won the Queen Mary Trophy at the R.N.R.S. Summer Show, the Silver-Gilt Flora Medal at the Royal Horticultural Society's Chelsea Show, and many Gold Medals up and down the country.

At the 1975 Summer Show of the R.N.R.S., Warley Rose Gardens won the China Trophy, a silver cup awarded to the best overall exhibit in Nurseryman's Class 2 (stands up to 300 square feet), for the thirteenth consecutive time. From its gardens beside Warley Street, south-west of Brentwood, this firm of growers supplies many varieties of roses and other kinds of plants. They have raised a number of outstanding rose varieties whose flowers bring pleasure to people living far beyond the bounds of Essex.

Admiral Rodney, a vigorous variety with large scented medium pink flowers flushed lighter at the centre, won the best bloom in show award at the 1975 Summer Show of the R.N.R.S. The variety takes its name from Admiral Lord Rodney whose victories in the eighteenth century included relieving Gibraltar, by defeating a Spanish squadron off Cape St Vincent, and crushing the French fleet off Dominica, and who, early in his career, had served on the Essex, one of the fleet in the Channel, and on Sheerness, a twenty-four-gun frigate. Hutton Village, another Warley rose introduction, com-

memorates the centenary of the rebuilding of All Saints'
Church in Hutton, now a suburb of Brentwood. Its scented
deep yellow flowers will surely delight countless lovers of the
rose.

The vine, another plant with a long history in Essex, is once
again being cultivated commercially in the county whose local
wines have already gained outstanding recognition, four different 'Felstar' wines having each won a Silver Award in the Club
Oenologique's International Wines and Spirits Competition
(1972-4). 'Felstar' is the registered trademark and the brand
name for the wines grown at Cricks Green, Felsted, about two
miles south-west of Braintree. Planting began in 1966 on a
gentle south-easterly slope whose soil is a heavy loam scattered
with flints, and where about 14,000 vines now grow in trellised
rows on the 10½-acre site.

The first wine was produced in 1969 and the highest yield to
date (1975) has been 9,000 bottles. 'Felstar', whose vineyard
was the first commercial one to be planted in Essex this
century, were the first in England to produce an 'Ice wine', the
fruit for this being gathered during a very heavy air frost in late
November or in December, usually at night, and pressed whilst
frozen. They have also produced Spätlese (late picked) and
Auslese (select late picked) wines in certain years. 'Felstar'
wines, white and rosé, are marketed under the varietal names
of the grapes from which they are produced, including Seyval
Blanc, Müller-Thurgau, Madeleine Sylvaner, and Madeleine
Angevine.

This is another large commercial-size vineyard at New Hall,
Purleigh, near Maldon, while a few small vineyards of half to
one and a half acres have been planted near Colchester.
Experience gained in these vineyards, large and small alike, has
confirmed that, despite a widespread belief to the contrary,
grapes can be produced in the open here. Contemporary
growers are, in fact, continuing a long, if interrupted tradition,
for vines were certainly grown in Roman Britain, and we
know from the Domesday account of Essex that there was
obviously great interest in grape-growing among the Normans
who established vineyards at Ashdon, Belchamp, Debden,
Great Waltham, Hedingham, Mundon, Rayleigh, Stambourne, Toppesfield, and Stebbing.

The willow growers of Essex may also be said to be following a long tradition, although, here again, its origin is obscure. Their crop, the cricket-bat willow, long regarded as a variety of the native white willow, is now considered by certain experts to have originated from a cross between the white willow and another species of willow. Be that as it may, there is no doubt that the cricket-bat willow is economically important in the county, especially in the area around Chelmsford. The graceful pyramidal trees are seen on fertile soil with an ample supply of moving water. Grown from big cuttings, 'sets' about eight feet high, they take from twelve to fifteen years (very occasionally as little as nine) to reach the girth of fifty inches required by bat makers who, like the cricketers themselves, value willow for its lightness and its great resistance to splitting.

Essex, where the proportion of woodland is low, is also the stronghold of another unusual tree, the hornbeam. Excellent as firewood and for the manufacture of charcoal, hornbeam is a useful, if very hard, timber. The smooth white wood is used for a number of specialist purposes, including chessmen, draughtsmen, mallets, and piano parts, but is of little real economic importance now.

Some years ago, the Forestry Commission acquired cleared woodlands near Saffron Walden and between Colchester and Chelmsford for re-planting, but the areas involved are very small compared with those managed by this body in, say, Norfolk and Suffolk. Forestry Commission grants have encouraged some private owners to plant trees, both hardwoods and conifers, but taxation, death duties, and lack of continuity in government policy discourage many from engaging in the long-term business of forestry. Despite such uncertainty, some outstanding tree-planters, men of vision, have gone ahead, often transforming woods ravaged in two world wars.

Colonel J. G. Round, who has dedicated more than half his woods for continual timber production, has planted thousands of oak, beech, pine, poplars and cricket-bat willows. On the banks of Hanningfield reservoir, a few miles south of Chelmsford, many thousands of poplar, beech, oak, pine and other trees have been planted over some 200 acres since 1960. Several people co-operated over this venture, which forms the subject of a twenty-minute film available from the Essex Water Company, including advisory officers of the Forestry Commission.

This official body is one of several organizations whose number includes the Agricultural Development and Advisory Service of the Ministry of Agriculture, Fisheries and Food, which advise those engaged in one or other of the various branches of agriculture, horticulture and forestry. And Essex is fortunate in having within its borders Writtle Agricultural College whose experience in preparing young people for entry to agriculture and horticulture is both long and successful. Founded in 1893, the College moved in 1940 from the centre of Chelmsford to its present site at Writtle, a property of 550 acres, comprising four farms, whose purchase four years earlier, at a time of mass unemployment and acute farming depression, showed outstanding foresight and courage on the part of the Essex County Council and the Ministry of Agriculture and Fisheries.

Now the college farms extend to 388 acres, covering four soil types. The arable section includes acreages of sugar beet, maincrop potatoes, winter wheat, barley, peas, and grain maize. Besides the pedigree British Friesians, with a herd average exceeding 1,300 gallons per cow, there are a crossbred sow pig herd and demonstration units for cereal-fed intensive beef and fat lamb production. Horticultural units demonstrate both commercial and amenity aspects and include fruit crops and the college's own packing station, glasshouses where tomatoes, cucumbers, roses, carnations, and other commercial crops are grown, and a plant nursery serving the needs of students interested in the commercial propagation and production of plants for sale. The college offers three year sandwich courses (six terms at college, three in industry) in agriculture and horticulture, as well as certain full-time courses of one term or one year. The Department of Extra-mural Studies offers day release, evening and short courses.

With residential accommodation for 200 of them, Writtle is well able to encourage its students, both men and women, to take a full and active interest in sporting, social and cultural activities organized by the Students' Union. The valuable work of this body in providing for the corporate life of the College was praised by the authors of an account of the seventy-five years of agricultural education in Essex from 1893 to 1968. A spokesman for the National Farmers' Union in Essex added his appreciation of the fact that Writtle: "produces not only good farmers and good technicians but also good leaders of men in a community that has need of them today."

The Young Farmers' Club movement in Essex (and indeed elsewhere) has, over the years, persistently encouraged young people to undertake leadership not only in their own clubs but also in the social and cultural life of the neighbourhood as a whole. There are sixteen Young Farmers' Clubs in Essex and four attached to schools, enabling about 1,000 members from both town and country to develop an active interest in rural life. Each club is completely self-administered and meets on one evening each week during the year. The atmosphere is friendly and informal, the programme varied, featuring activities that may be entertaining, sporting or educational. Many members have taken advantage of opportunities to represent their clubs on the county organizing body and in various competitions at both county and national levels, to take part in exchange visits to other parts of Britain, and to travel abroad.

Essex Young Farmer, the lively bi-monthly journal of the Essex County Federation of Young Farmers' Clubs, helps to keep clubs and members in touch with one another, giving news and dates of forthcoming events. Its first issue of the year arrived recently and, while finishing this chapter, I have read not only of bonfire parties and Christmas celebrations but also about Essex Young Farmers who took part in National Sheep, Beef, and Dairy Stock Judging Competitions, the Essex girl who, as a non-farming member of Chelmsford Young Farmers' Club, was placed first in the Intermediate Section of the National Dairy Stock Judging Competition, and those members who came first in a quiz contest at Writtle Agricultural College against present and past students and agricultural merchants.

The great county event of the year for Essex Young Farmers must surely be their annual show and rally, an all-day event ending with a show dance. As a former leader of two Young Farmers' Clubs attached to schools, one in Sussex, the other in Oxfordshire, I find great satisfaction in the fact that the show and rally schedule provides some twenty classes for school clubs, embracing domestic, art and craft, and livestock competitions. The main classes encourage entries from members engaged in a wide range of activities, making an item of basket work or a portrait in charcoal, open fat-lamb judging, dairy calves, Scottish dancing – to mention but a few of nearly fifty classes.

With many more classes than the Young Farmers' Show, the Essex County Show is an annual two-day event held in June at the Essex Agricultural Society's permanent showground at Great Leighs, eight miles from Chelmsford. Many breeds of horses, ponies, cattle, goats and pigs are exhibited and judged, there is a flower show, numerous trade stands attract attention, and an element of real action and excitement derives from the driving classes and jumping competitions. The Essex Agricultural Society, whose objects are to further agriculture and all related trades, crafts and interests, and to hold an annual agricultural show or shows, was formed in 1858 under its original name of Essex Agricultural Association. Its first show was held at Chelmsford in the same year and 2,567 people visited the one-day event. In 1974 the total attendance at the show, a two-day event since 1868, was over 65,000.

For many people one of the great pleasures of the county show is the sight of so many horses and ponies. The heavy breeds – Shires, Suffolks, and Percherons – always seem to attract special attention, possibly because of the memories they revive of former times when very few farms were worked without horses. The Suffolk was always a farmer's horse, but many of those seeing it now, with its lively chestnut colour, arched crest, fine silky mane, and short neck, may find difficulty in appreciating the important part once played by this tireless worker on the land, in peace and war alike, and as a heavy battery horse for artillery work during the First World War. Certainly it reminds us that, like war, agriculture has undergone considerable, almost unbelievable, changes, events in which Essex has been to the fore.

VIII

INDUSTRY

ALTHOUGH, as we have already seen, the county is, and has long been, an important centre of agriculture and horticulture, Essex has made an important contribution to the industrial achievements of Britain, not least in the vital field of exports. Certain of the old county industries, involving the processing or production of food, drink and building materials, survive, albeit often on a different scale or in a different form. The necessity of salt for direct human consumption and for the preservation of fish and meat led our ancestors to take considerable interest in the manufacture of this substance in Essex. Much of the salt used now comes from other parts of Britain, but salt-making by the evaporation of sea water is still carried on at Maldon. Here the Maldon Crystal Salt Company, the only producers of British sea salt, makes Maldon table sea salt whose attractive flavour and crystal form are appreciated by customers in Britain, Europe and the United States.

As is the case with malting, mentioned in chapter seven, the brewing industry has undergone considerable change in recent times. Indeed there is only one brewery left in Essex, that of T. D. Ridley and Sons (Brewers) Limited at Hartford End in the depths of the countryside. Mr N. Ridley, director of the company, to whom I am greatly indebted for information, tells me that within the brewery there is a mash tun of ten quarters capacity, and also a steam coil copper sufficient to take the volume of ninety barrels. Ten old wooden fermenting vessels, each of fifty-barrel size, are still in use, having been lined with copper. Ridleys bottle about half of their output, using equipment capable of dealing with 9,000 bottles per hour.

They use wooden casks exclusively for their draught beer from the wood, probably their strongest selling feature. Besides pale ale (draught bitter from the wood), Ridley's products are mild (dark mild), stout (non-sweet stout), Essex Brown (a normal brown ale), Essex Light (light ale), Old Bob (strong pale ale), Stock (strong dark ale), and Bishops Ale, a barley wine naturally conditioned prior to bottling. Mr Ridley tells me that, as far as he knows, the company has not won any awards, but that their customers seem happy with their beer so far. Their products meet with the approval of CAMRA, the Campaign for Real Ale, who favour the traditional English pub and traditional English beer served without gas! Certainly it is always a great pleasure to me to drink Ridley's ale not only in Essex but also in Cambridge where I live during CAMRA's annual Beer Festival, which is held in the old corn exchange in the very heart of the town.

The industry of distilling, for which Colchester was once a main centre, is carried on at Harlow by International Distillers and Vintners. They produce gin from ingredients obtained in Britain and from Germany and Italy.

Flour-milling, another old Essex industry, is still undertaken at Chelmsford and Colchester and at other places in the county. Some Essex mills, particularly the older ones, are in attractive settings. At Dedham on the Stour the present mill, a large brick building, stands on the site of the mill owned by Golding Constable, miller, merchant and farmer, whose son, the celebrated John Constable, painted several versions of *Dedham Lock and Mill*. By the way, anyone going to Dedham should also visit Castle House, the home for many years of Sir Alfred Munnings, former President of the Royal Academy, many of whose paintings and drawings are exhibited there. He is often thought of elsewhere for his outspoken comments on certain aspects of modern art, but here, in Constable Country, he is remembered as a great character who loved horses, the subjects of many of his works, and who really cared for such details of the countryside as the state of a neglected footbridge or stile. Munnings was born at Mendham in neighbouring Suffolk, the miller's son, a fact which may perhaps excuse my mentioning him here!

The manufacture of bricks and tiles also has a long history in Essex. The Romans made these building materials and examples of their work may be seen in Colchester and elsewhere. Brick-making appears to have died out for a time, being reintroduced from Flanders early in the thirteenth century. Nowadays Essex reds are among the products of Milton Hall (Southend) Brick Company, makers of facing bricks since 1878, while 'specials' of varying shapes and sizes for use in restoration of historic monuments are made by the Bulmer Brick and Tile Company at their works between Gestingthorpe and Bulmer Tye. Cement-making has long been carried on at the southern edge of the county, beside the Thames at Grays and Thurrock, and it is here, too, that aerated concrete is produced in huge steam autoclaves.

Boats have been built in Essex for countless generations and they are still made at Burnham-on-Crouch, Brightlingsea, Maldon, and several other places on the coast, and inland, at Witham, where fibreglass and plastic hulls for yachts and similar craft are produced by Ardleigh Laminated Plastics. Sail Craft of Brightlingsea produce 'Tornados', international-class catamarans, whose use in Olympic racing has earned them an outstanding reputation.

Printing is another industry that has long been important here. Widespread, with hundreds of small firms and with larger concerns operating in such places as Southend, Wickford, and Benfleet, it, too, carries the name of Essex far beyond its borders. The county's two new towns have benefited from the arrival of printers from London, and the establishment of such associated industries as book binding and the manufacture of printing inks and printing machinery has also provided employment. Nowadays, with such a vast quantity being generated, much printed matter soon ends up as waste paper. This important raw material is recycled at Purfleet, on Thamesside, where various forms of paperboard are made for conversion into cartons, book covers, tubes and numerous other types of packaging.

The making of textiles has provided employment in Essex for centuries, and the former prosperity of such places as Coggeshall and Dedham resulted largely from this industry. Today one recalls with pride that Courtaulds, whose name and products are known throughout the world, was wholly Essex-based until the late nineteenth century. The family firm was effectively created in 1816 when Samuel Courtauld III set up on his own account as a silk throwster in Bocking, the next parish to Braintree. In 1819, young Courtauld, now aged twenty-six, leased a water-powered mill at Bocking, and six years later converted the former corn mill in the neighbouring town of Halstead. His brother, George Courtauld II, ran the engineering side of the business. This was responsible for the design and manufacture of almost all the firm's machinery, and there is no doubt that mechanization was a vital factor in the prosperous growth of Courtaulds whose capital grew from just over £40,000 to more than £450,000, and whose annual profits rocketed from £3,000 to £110,000, in the half-century 1835-85.

Later, Samuel Courtauld and Company found itself in difficulties caused by changes in the British economy, failure of business leadership, and its dependence on the sale of the once-fashionable mourning crape. It was felt that the Essex firm was remote from the major textile areas of the Midlands and North, but this isolation ended in 1898, the year a mill was bought at Leigh in Lancashire. Six years later, in July 1904, the company acquired the exclusive British rights to the 'viscose' process of making rayon (artificial silk), the first of the man-made fibres. A factory to work the new process was built at Coventry, but its products were subjected to tests and experiments at Courtauld's Essex mills and application of the results obtained there helped the firm to triumph over all its foreign rivals.

Since the early days in Essex, Courtaulds have continued to evolve. Companies of the group are now engaged in the manufacture and processing of fibres, fabrics, chemicals and plastics, and engineering. Samuel Courtauld and Company undertake weaving at Braintree and Halstead (and at four more centres in other parts of England), processing at Braintree, and dyeing and finishing at Bocking. At Braintree lining materials are woven from Tricel and Dicel yarns, and lining cloths for ladies' wear are exported in large quantities. Here, too, Tricel yarn is twisted for weaving at other Samuel Courtauld mills into fabrics. At Halstead mill, where Courtaulds' first rayon yarns were woven in 1906, is the group's largest water jet weaving plant. Much of the fabric produced there is exported. The principal cloths are Celon taffeta for use in anoraks, sleeping bags and linings, and Tricel georgette for dresswear. In addition, Elastomeric yarn is woven for use in the French corsetry trade. As exporters, Samuel Courtauld and Co. Ltd. have undoubtedly helped to earn the two Queen's Awards for exports won by Courtaulds Limited, of which it is a subsidiary.

In various parts of Essex, clothing manufacturers continue an industry which earlier played an important part in the economic life of the Colchester district. Today, at Billericay, L. S. and J. Sussman Ltd, a company founded in London in 1889, make the famous St Michael shirt for Marks and Spencer, while in Harwich is the factory of Bernard and Sons Ltd, leading tailors in naval and service uniforms. At Basildon, Ben Williams and Co. Ltd, manufacturers of men's and youths' outerwear, have pioneered the use of a highly engineered Swedish overhead conveyor system. Harlow has attracted dressmaking, fashion rainwear, and other clothing firms, and there are makers of dresses and suits on Canvey Island.

At East Tilbury, at the southern extremity of the county, is the manufacturing complex of the British Bata Shoe Company whose many ranges of footwear include the popular Marbot Essex men's and boys' shoes. Close to the administration building is a statue of Tomas Bata, the founder, whose Bata Shoe Organisation now includes ninety-eight companies in eighty-nine countries, 5,000 Bata-owned retail stores, and five engineering works, employs more than 84,000 people, and produces almost 240 million pairs of shoes each year. Born into a family of shoemakers, Bata, a man of vision, determination and compassion, founded the original company at Zlin, Czechoslovakia, in 1894. He was then only eighteen years old! In 1932, the year Tomas Bata died in an air crash, the Bata Shoe Organization bought land at East Tilbury where the first shoes – textile shoes with leather soles and rubber plimsolls, came off the machines in the first single-storey factory in July of the following year. Building continued and in 1939 a complex of four five-storey units was completed. These housed the leather factory, the rubber factory, the administration and service departments, and the hotel where staff or visiting customers could stay. In addition, 400 houses, a number of shops, a swimming-pool, tennis courts, and a sports field were provided for staff accommodation and amenities.

Other developments have since taken place at East Tilbury, one of which was the setting up of the associate company, Power Sportshoes. Now, in 1976, as it marks the one hundredth anniversary of its founder's birth, the Bata Organisation can point with pride to its achievements in Essex, not least to its efforts in the field of exports.

Unlike footwear production, engineering is widespread in Essex. Many firms involved are small, but the value of their service to industry should not be underestimated. Others are bigger, employing more people, and it is largely from these that I have selected examples.

The Hoffmann Works at Chelmsford was the second of the new factories built during the industrial expansion of the town at the very end of last century (the first, that of Colonel Crompton, eminent pioneering electrical engineer, is now partly occupied by a Marconi company). Ernst Gustaf Hoffmann, a Swiss-American engineer who held patents relating to the production of precision steel balls, had joined members of the Barrett family in establishing the Hoffmann Manufacturing Company there in 1898. The increased demand for ball bearings during the First World War resulted in the Hoffmann Works almost doubling in size. Between the wars, the company supplied bearings to most of the main engineering concerns, and during the Second World War, when it also operated two dispersal plants in other parts of Britain, it was busily engaged on work of considerable national importance. In 1969, the merger of the three leading British bearing manufacturers made Hoffmann part of Ransome Hoffmann Pollard Limited (RHP). The works at Chelmsford were linked with works at Newark to form the General Bearings Division of RHP, now one of the world's largest rolling bearing manufacturers.

It is not easy for the layman to keep pace with such mergers and other forms of industrial reorganisation, but it is always pleasing to find Essex companies making important contributions towards the activities of larger parent-groups. Such was the case when enquiries about the Chelmsford Tool and Gauge Company, whose factory is on the Widford Hall Industrial Estate at Chelmsford, revealed that it is now one of the engineering manufacturing companies of the Myson Group, designers and manufacturers of heating, ventilating and air conditioning equipment, which is sold not only for residential and commercial purposes, but also for use in marine, agricultural, mining, petrochemical, food processing, paper and textile industries. With the merchant division at Ongar, where the company, now an international organization, was started as recently as 1953, and its air distribution, agricultural, and export sales divisions at Colchester, the group is well represented in Essex, where (to give but one example of their export orders) Myson Fans (Colchester) have collaborated with Myson A.B. (Sweden) to develop a pump room fan for extracting contaminated air from the holds of ocean-going tankers.

The vast Marconi organization has long shown a vital concern for safety and communications at sea and these remain among their many interests. Essex was indeed fortunate when, in December 1898, a building, formerly a silk factory and furniture warehouse, in Hall Street, Chelmsford, was acquired by the Wireless Telegraph and Signal Company Limited, the company formed to develop Guglielmo Marconi's apparatus for wireless telegraphy commercially, whose name became Marconi's Wireless Telegraph Co. Ltd, and later still The Marconi Company Ltd.

There has been much discussion as to why Chelmsford was chosen, but suffice it to say that the Hall Street premises became the first wireless factory in the world. In 1901 the company opened the world's first wireless school at Frinton to supplement the students' engineering knowledge with the principles and practice of Marconi wireless. By 1911 the Hall Street works were inadequate and the following year new and larger workshops and laboratories (the first purpose-built radio factory in the world) were opened at New Street, Chelmsford. W. J. Baker, in *A History of The Marconi Company* (Methuen, 1970), tells the story of the company's advance up to 1965, and readers are referred to this excellent book for details of the many 'firsts' with which the company is associated, including Britain's first advertised public broadcast programme, which was made from Marconi's works in Chelmsford on 15th June 1920, the first regular sound broadcasting service in Britain (1922), and the provision of transmission equipment for the world's first television service (1936).

Following the important merger between GEC and English Electric in 1968, several major capital electronics interests were brought together under the aegis of a great new company, GEC-Marconi Electronics Ltd. The result is an international organization of associated and subsidiary companies, augmented by a network of indigenous representative organizations and GEC-Marconi technical representatives, covering virtually every country in the world.

The GEC-Marconi Electronics headquarters is at Chelmsford where there are establishments of Marconi Communication Systems Ltd, Marconi Radar Systems Ltd, The Marconi International Marine Co. Ltd, and Coastal Radio Ltd. Here, too, is Marconi College, where, in the past ten years, engineers from more than fifty countries have been trained. Marconi Communication Systems Ltd also maintains establishments at Writtle and Billericay, while Marconi-Elliott Avionic Systems Ltd, the company dealing with avionics design and production and certain missile and industrial activities, has one of its four major establishments at Basildon. The GEC-Marconi Electronic research laboratories at Great Baddow are unique in the industry. There, supported by a comprehensive computer facility, engineers investigate new materials and devices, problems associated with the uses and inter-connection of microcircuits, and many other matters.

It was in the Baddow research laboratories that the Marconi valve section was started early in the Second World War. Soon more machines, staff and space were needed to produce magnetrons used in modernizing airborne radar for the Royal Air Force and the section moved to Waterhouse Lane, Chelmsford, which, since 1947, has been the base of the English Electric Valve Co. Ltd. Founded from the wartime Marconi valve laboratories, EEV, a member of the GEC group of companies, is now Europe's leading company designing and manufacturing specialized electronic components for use in radar, broadcasting, television, medicine, education, and industry. In 1961 the parts manufacturing section was transferred from Waterhouse Lane, a site now about ten times larger than it was in 1947, to Maldon. Then, in 1967, transfer of the cathode-ray section from Chelmsford to Benfleet was completed. EEV has twice won the Queen's Award for technology (for image isocons in 1968 and for ceramic hydrogen thyratrons in 1973), and the sale of almost 75 per cent of their products overseas not only helps in the vital task of increasing British exports but must also advance the international reputation of our engineering skills.

Standard Telephones and Cables Limited (STC), an important British company operating in the field of international communications, has been associated with south-east Essex since 1964, equipment for networks carrying telephone messages and television pictures across the world being designed and manufactured in their factories at Benfleet and Basildon.

The completion of the Ford Tractor Plant at Basildon early in 1964 was notable, locally as a source of employment for some 3,000 people, nationally as a large producer of tractors and service parts (over 80 per cent of British-made tractors and parts are exported), and internationally as a factor in agricultural mechanization, a stark necessity in the more heavily populated and under-developed parts of the world. At the end of 1963, Ford, the first company to manufacture tractors in quantity in Britain, began to run down production of Fordson tractors at Dagenham and the last one (the 1,159,365th!) came off the line there towards the end of the following year. At the Basildon plant, one of two new factories built to replace the old tractor factory at Dagenham (the other is at Antwerp), skilled workers make engines, front suspensions and hydraulic lift components for all Ford tractors throughout the world and assemble Ford tractors for sale in every country in the world except the U.S.A. and those of the European Common Market. Each day some 500 engines, hydraulics and front suspensions are produced and 300 tractors assembled.

The founder of the Ford empire, Henry Ford (King Henry I of Industry), the American farmer's son who hated the drudgery of farming in his youth, had made his first tractor, an experimental model, in 1907. More than a century earlier, an Essex farmer, William Bentall of Goldhanger, the ancient village on the Blackwater, became a full-time maker of agricultural implements, producing 'Goldhanger' ploughs based on the patterns of one he had designed for his own farm. He moved a few miles in 1805 to new buildings at Heybridge where Bentalls have been ever since and where the present company, a division of ACROW, opened their large modern works as recently as October 1974. Nowadays Bentalls are leading specialists in the manufacture of grain handling, storage and conditioning plants, provender machinery for preparing animal feed, and automatic feed systems. It is pleasing to see that the name of Goldhanger is associated with their drying and storage silos. Exports, now accounting for about 40 per cent of their turnover, have long been important to Bentalls. Recently this fact was emphasized by that delightful monthly magazine *Essex Countryside* which published a reader's photographs of machinery made by the company at "Heybridge, Maldon, England" and now lying half-buried opposite her home in New Zealand.

R. Hunt and Co. Ltd of Atlas Works, Earls Colne, another old-established Essex company, export about 35 per cent of their production of agricultural machinery and mechanical power transmission equipment, mainly to developing countries. Founded in the early 1820s by Robert Hunt, a millwright from Soham in Cambridgeshire, on the site where the present works stand, it now employs some 300 people in the woodshop, pattern shop, foundry, machine shop, tool room, fitting shop and other sections. Still very much a family business, Hunts is a vitally important source of work in Earls Colne. For many years the company has taken an active part in the life of the village where it has built thirty-three Homes of Rest for the elderly and some 140 houses, bungalows and flats, which are let to full-time employees, company pensioners and their widows at reasonable rents. Visitors to the church, observing the pew ends carved with representatives of Hunts' products, are reminded of other worthy acts of the firm and the family.

Crittall Windows Ltd, operating at Braintree, Witham and Silver End (which is between the other two places), produce standard and purpose made windows in aluminium and galvanized steel. This company is one of several created during the reorganization of Crittall-Hope after its acquisition by the Norcros group in 1974. The formation of Crittall-Hope in 1965 had resulted from a merger of the two largest window producing companies in Britain – Crittall Manufacturing

Company, whose first factory was built at Manor Street, Braintree, in 1893, and Henry Hope and Sons Ltd of Smethwick. Essex folk must be pleased that the present company bears the name of Crittall, for the family did much for the county, providing employment and building at Silver End a complete village, including 500 houses, the window fittings factory, and many amenities.

The annals of Essex are rich in similar examples of individuals, families and companies who have contributed in their own particular ways to our industrial history. Writing in 1976, centenary year of the Paxman Works at the Hythe, Colchester, one salutes the memory of James Paxman (1832-1922), whose name is now borne by Paxman Diesels Ltd, a management company of GEC Diesels Ltd. Born at Colchester, James Paxman left school at the age of fifteen to learn a trade in his father's smithy, fitting and wheelwright's shop at Elmstead. Within five years he was Works Manager of an engineering and iron founding company in his native town, and in 1865 became a partner in Davey, Paxman and Davey, engineers. This company flourished and moved into a new factory on the site of the present Paxman Works in 1876. At the time of his death, Paxman was one of Britain's leading civil engineers, a distinguished and generous citizen of Colchester, and head of Davey, Paxman and Company (as the firm was then known), one of whose characteristic features was, as *The Producer,* a Co-operative Society publication, put it, "a regard for the workpeople and the townsfolk of Colchester."

Paxman's ingenuity and attention to detail were inherited and applied by his son Edward, who died in 1949. There is no member of the family in the business now. But the traditional high standards of engineering are upheld, and export orders are still treated with the care and attention they received from James Paxman almost a century ago, a fact acknowledged when the firm received the Queen's Award for exports.

Now, with a site almost twice the size of the original eleven acres and a workforce that has increased from about 200 to 2,200, Paxmans produce diesel engines (from 274 to 4,000 horsepower) and process plant equipment for food and confectionery manufacturers, breweries, oil refineries, the mining industry and sewage treatment works. They are currently

Colchester Castle

Chelmsford, the shopping centre

Coastal erosion at Walton-on-the-Naze

Coast protection at Walton-on-the-Naze

Headquarters of the Essex Naturalists Trust,
Fingringhoe Wick

Swans, shipping and maltings at Mistley

Funfair and pier at Clacton-on-Sea

The busy port of Harwich *L*

The church and inn at Great Waltham

Churchend and church of St Mary, Great Dunmow

Town Street from the ancient guildhall, Thaxted

Chapel Street, Billericay

Cereal crops near Thaxted

Harvesting beans near Saffron Walden

All Saints' Church, Stock

All Saints' Church, Norton Mandeville

producing engines for the Ministry of Defence, Navy, and British Rail's high-speed trains, the prototype of which, powered by two Paxman Valenta engines, each developing 2,250 horse power at 1,500 revolutions per minute, took the world speed record for a diesel-hauled train by achieving 230 kilometres per hour (143 miles per hour).

Paxmans are also making engines that will be used for various duties in many parts of the world. (They supply diesel engines to forty-two navies of the world). Their long and extensive connection with the oil industry has included provision of diesel engines for 'Sea Quest', the offshore drilling rig associated with the discovery of North Sea oil in Forties field, and the Forties platforms which produced the very first North Sea oil to be pumped ashore.

The most southerly part of Essex, on Thamesside, is an important centre for the storage and refining of imported oil. Each year at Coryton millions of tons of crude oil are processed into petrol, fuel and diesel oils, petroleum gases and other substances. Many such products are also made at Purfleet where, as at Shellhaven, chemicals are produced as by-products of the oil industry.

New high quality synthetic rubber sheetings were becoming available in 1965, and that year Butyl Products was incorporated for the specific purpose of developing their use. Today, with factories in Billericay, France and South Africa, the group forms the world's largest fabricator of hydraulic membranes. The installation of these linings in water and chemical storage projects is undertaken or supervized in many parts of the world by the company's specialist technicians.

In 1970 the company was given the Queen's Award for exports, 60 per cent of its materials being exported at present. One very interesting project carried out in Britain was the laying of Butyl rubber sheeting (1.5 millimetres thick) over the floor of a sixteen-acre settlement reservoir at Northern Burway, Chertsey. In 1968 it was estimated that the cost saving achieved by using this synthetic rubber instead of reinforced concrete amounted to some £190,000. One of the many projects undertaken overseas was a 1,000,000 gallon Gi-tank, a giant flexible container, prefabricated in the Billericay factory and then installed into an excavation in

Africa to make covered storage for potable water.

Cigarette manufacturing is another Essex industry with vital international connections, the modern establishment of Carreras Rothmans Ltd at Basildon being one of the busiest cigarette factories in the world. Tobacco is brought there daily from bonded stores at London, Liverpool and Manchester docks, blended, processed and made into cigarettes whose leading brands include Rothmans King Size (the world's largest-selling king-size Virginia filter cigarette), Piccadilly, Guards, Consulate, Dunhill and Rothmans International. Each year 75 per cent of the hundreds of millions of Essex-made cigarettes are exported to 160 different markets in more than 1,000 different packagings. About 2,600 people are employed at Basildon to make, pack and ship them. The history of their employers, Carreras Rothmans Ltd, now the wholly owned United Kingdom subsidiary of Rothmans International, can be traced back to two men – Jose Joaquin Carreras, son of a Spanish nobleman, and Louis Rothman, a London-based Ukrainian immigrant.

Yardley, another great company that came to Basildon from London, has historical associations with Essex through members of the family who for generations were lords of the manor in the Thaxted area. Long famous for perfumes, cosmetics and fine soaps, the Yardley companies together form a world-wide corporation. Three companies operate from England, but only Yardley Basildon concerns us here. The factory at Basildon was constructed on a nineteen-acre site, the production, warehousing and development areas, together with the four-storey office block, occupying some eleven acres. Hundreds of different products are manufactured there, many for sale in this country but another 200 to 300 types for international markets like South America, the Middle and Far East, Europe, and Eastern European countries. Over the years Yardley have received a number of awards for their products. Recently the company won a gold medal for the second time running at the Brno Industrial Consumer Goods Trade Fair in Czechoslovakia, a unique achievement by any firm.

The products of many other Essex companies take the county's name across the world. From Brentwood, Thermos Limited, winners of the Queen's Award to Industry and one of the world's largest vacuum flask companies, export vacuum vessels of many kinds. Also in Brentwood is the factory where Selo Limited produce about eighty different types of photographic film, ranging from x-ray film to colour film and meeting the needs of the radiologist, both professional and amateur photographers, and the cinematograph industry. Connected with Selo Limited are Ilford Limited who produce processing chemicals, spools and cassettes at their large plant at Basildon. This new town also includes among its manufacturers Spong and Company Limited, makers of domestic kitchenware, pot scourers and knitted wire, and wireworkers to the car and related industries. With some 600,000 of these useful gadgets being produced each year, Spong mincers have become world famous.

And so one could go on, for the record and achievements of Essex industry are most impressive. One may not always be pleased with the visual impact or other results of industrial development, but one must never underestimate the importance of industry's contribution to the economy of Britain and indeed the very life of this heavily populated country.

IX

NATURE IN ESSEX

T RUE lovers of nature regard the flowers of even our most abundant plants as things of beauty. They enjoy the presence of common birds and other creatures in their gardens, often going to considerable trouble to provide them with food, water and nesting boxes. To these people red valerian growing on ancient walls in Colchester and elsewhere is not only an attractive species but one of an amazing number and variety of living organisms, some common and widespread, others rare and of local distribution, whose presence adds to the quality of human life. Essex has produced many such nature-lovers. Some have published learned books and papers, but others – far more numerous – have been content simply to enjoy nature in their own quiet and modest way, leaving no books or collections as individual memorials.

Naturalists who do aspire to distinction have before them the excellent example of John Ray, "the greatest of all field naturalists", whose biographer, Charles Raven, wrote:

> His greatness is that in a time of transition and universal turmoil he saw the need for precise and ordered knowledge, set himself to test the old and explore the new, and by dint of immense labour in the field and in the study laid the foundations of modern science in the many branches of zoology and botany.

John Ray, son of the village blacksmith, was born in 1627 at Black Notley where he died in 1705. After attending Braintree Grammar School he entered Cambridge, being elected a Fellow of Trinity College in 1649. Nine years later Ray made the first of his botanical excursions of England and Wales. Travel on the Continent, to study the flora of Western Europe, was made possible by the help of friends when Ray, a dissenter, had to resign his Fellowship on the coming into force of the Act of Uniformity.

Nowadays the great libraries treasure his books, especially his *Historia Plantarum* (History of plants), a systematic arrangement of all the then known plants. In London the learned Ray Society bears his name, and one of the Braintree schools is thus distinguished. An obelisk commemorating him stands in a delightful spot just south of the nave of Black Notley church, away from the road but close to the hall and its big fifteenth-century barn. Next to the monument is the table-tomb of Benjamin Allen, the Braintree naturalist and physician who claimed to have cured his friend John Ray of jaundice by giving him an infusion of stallion's dung in beer.

Medical science had discarded such remedies by 1862 when George Stacey Gibson published his *Flora of Essex*, the first such work to cover the whole county. Gibson, who was born in Saffron Walden in 1818, developed a love of plants early in life, adding several species to the British flora while still in his twenties. The son of Wyatt George Gibson, the banker and brewer, he became mayor of his native town and one of its great benefactors. He replaced the eighteenth-century red-brick town hall by a new one in a 'Tudor' style whose half-timbered gable struck Sir Nikolaus Pevsner as ostentatious and coarse. His generosity enabled the Friends' School to move to Saffron Walden and when, largely as the result of this, the congregation attending the Quaker Meeting increased in size he enlarged the Meeting House in High Street. Saffron Walden museum also benefited by his gifts of money and natural history and archaeological collections. The Gibson's family home, 75 High Street, survives in Saffron Walden, a friendly little town where one always seems to be close to the countryside.

Gibson's county flora was not replaced for more than a century, until, in fact, the Essex Naturalists' Trust (an excellent body about which we shall have more to say later) issued a new *Flora of Essex* in 1974. Its author, Stanley Thomas Jermyn, had died suddenly towards the end of the previous year, but what a magnificent memorial this book is! How hard he worked to create this account of 1,733 species, sub-species, varieties and hybrids, visiting many times and at different seasons of the year each of the fifty-seven ten kilometre squares into which the National Grid divides Essex. But work was no stranger to Stanley Jermyn who, born at Benfleet in 1909, the seventh of ten children, started to make his own way in the world at the age of fourteen, rising from clerk to traffic manager.

He devoted his leisure to natural history, especially botany, and joined the Essex Naturalists' Trust when it was founded in 1959, eventually serving as its General Secretary and Treasurer until his death. Jermyn expressed great concern over the adverse effects of changes in the Essex countryside on plants and other forms of wild life, naming loss of habitats due to land development, changed methods of farming and forestry, chemical sprays and drainage of wetlands among the destructive forces involved. Nevertheless, as one of many distinguished successors to William Turner, "the father of English botany", whose *Herball* of 1562 included records of Essex plants, he pinned his faith on "the ever growing awareness among the population that there is a real and urgent need to preserve natural things".

The history of Essex ornithology does not appear to have begun until 1666 when Christopher Merrett reported the occurrence in the county of the rare and exotic hoopoe. Notes and articles about Essex birds did not appear in any number until the nineteenth-century when, in 1890, Miller Christy published his *Birds of Essex*. Born near Chelmsford, this distinguishing Essex antiquary acquired his great love of nature while attending the Quaker school at Epping. His book was superseded by W. E. Glegg's *A History of the Birds of Essex* in 1929, but Miller Christy is remembered as one of the founders of the Essex Field Club and one who showed considerable foresight in industrial archaeology. Broomwood, the half-timbered and gabled house built for him by Fred Rowntree, still graces Chignal.

Like so many of his fellow countrymen before and since, William Edwin Glegg left his native Scotland and came south as a young man. Although he never actually resided here, he was very fond of Essex and tramped its length and breadth in preparation for his book on the county's birds, retaining his interest and affection throughout the remainder of his life. An

ornithologist of international repute, William Glegg, already a
Permanent Vice-President of the Essex Field Club, greeted
with enthusiasm the formation of the Essex Bird-watching and
Preservation Society, becoming its first President in 1949.

Formed to cover the whole of the county, the young Society
produced its first annual *Essex Bird Report*. Deciding that a new
history was needed to replace Glegg's work, it issued, as an
interim measure, *A Guide to the birds of Essex* in 1968. This
included details of the status and distribution of 297 full species,
of which 123 had actually bred in Essex during the previous
twenty-five years or so. The *Guide* chronicles the spread in
Essex, following its appearance there in 1957, of the collared
dove whose first British nest was discovered at Cromer,
Norfolk, in 1955, and reports the increase of jays, great spotted
woodpeckers, and certain other birds. But it also treats of the
realities of bird life in the county when mentioning decreases of
such species as barn owl, cuckoo, and sparrowhawk.

In turning to other forms of wildlife whose diversity has
aroused the interest of Essex naturalists we give pride of place
to insects, some of which are subjects of *A Guide to the
Butterflies and larger Moths of Essex*. Compiled by seven Essex
entomologists, who dealt with some 12,000 records of these
insects, and published in 1975 by the Essex Naturalists' Trust,
this book pays tribute to many of those who have contributed
to Essex entomology over past decades, years during which
great changes have taken place in the composition of the
county's butterfly and moth fauna. As with so many other
organisms, these insects have suffered considerably from destruction and disturbance of habitats. But, even so, the new
Guide includes 635 species, about two-thirds of the British
macrolepidoptera.

The celebrated John Ray, whose achievements were mentioned earlier, studied insects collected near his Essex home
and others sent to him by friends and correspondents. His
descriptions of a purple emperor captured by a Mr Courtman
at Castle Hedingham and a white admiral taken by a Mr
Morton near Tollesbury formed the first published accounts
of these butterflies. Sadly Ray did not live to see the publication of his *Historia Insectorum* (History of Insects). Issued in
1710, five years after his death, it includes forty-seven British

butterflies, many mentioned for the first time.

During the first half of the nineteenth century Dr Alan Maclean, a Colchester physician, invented a special butterfly net – 'Maclean's elastic net', and Henry Doubleday, an Epping grocer, started to attract moths by brushing 'sugar-water' on the bark of trees, his brother Edward having observed how moths were attracted to empty sugar barrels. Later that century William Harwood, the Colchester entomologist and natural history dealer, perfected the technique of sleeving – rearing larvae in muslin sleeves on growing foodplants.

Another distinguished Essex entomologist, Gervase Frederick Mathew, former District Paymaster to the Harwich Coast-guard District, had published more than 300 notes and papers on insects by the time he died in 1928. His name was given to Mathew's Wainscot, a local moth of coastal districts, which he discovered on salt marshes at Dovercourt, where it still occurs, in 1895.

Over the years other Essex naturalists have taken an active part in the study of butterflies and moths and many more types of insects. Not only does this tradition continue here but it is steadily embracing a praise-worthy emphasis on the conserv-ation of insects and their habitats. One is pleased to add that, in what is often regarded as an age of professionals, there is still room for the amateur. Take the wonderful example of Frederick Buck who died early in 1975. This eminent amateur entomologist was General Manager of the Anchor Press, Tiptree, whose fine work carries the name of Essex throughout the world (See, for example, their magnificent printing of David Jasen's biography of P. G. Wodehouse, which was beautifully bound by Wm Brendon and Son Ltd, also of Tiptree). Yet he will be remembered in the world of natural history as a leading national authority on beetles, as the author of a handbook published by the Royal Entomological Society of London (of which he was a Fellow) and of many scientific papers, as editor of the transactions of natural history societies which he also served in various other capacities in Essex and elsewhere, and for many other reasons.

The activities of entomologists here have resulted in the name of Essex itself being borne by the Essex skipper butterfly and the Essex emerald, a beautiful pale green moth. Common on parts of the county's coast, the first-named also occurs in several inland localities. The Essex emerald is in a completely different category, for in Britain it is confined to the Essex salt marshes and very rare. The activities of collectors have proved to be very harmful to it and it has also suffered from the destruction of its foodplant, sea wormwood. Much to their credit, members of the Essex Naturalists' Trust decided to seek the moth's protection under the Conservation of Wild Creatures and Wild Plants Act 1975 soon after this legislation was passed.

In Essex, as in so many other places, mammals have not always received the serious attention of naturalists. That great son of Essex John Ray left an important systematic treatise on mammals and snakes, much of which was adopted by Carl Linnaeus, the eighteenth-century Swedish biologist whose *Systema Naturae* (tenth edition) forms the very foundation of all systematic zoology. In the 1930s Arthur Thompson, the natural history writer and photographer who lived at Coggeshall in Essex for a time, was something of a pioneer of nature conservation. He advocated legal protection for the otter. This interesting and playful animal was, he said, becoming rarer. Now we know how right he was. He wanted naturalists to pay close and careful attention to bats, useful insect-eaters, but in many quarters they are almost as little-known now as then. Leaving the mammals for a while, one remembers Thompson urging people not to destroy frogs, toads and other amphibians, and hears again the strong things he said about those who killed owls.

Many of the creatures suffering persecution forty years ago are still threatened even now, in the 1970s, some more so than ever before. The creation of nature reserves and other war-dened areas is doing something to ease the problem in Essex. But it is becoming obvious that many more of these places are needed, as are more people prepared to work as volunteers in the reserves themselves and in the wider area of conservation education.

An important development in this latter field was the establishment in European Conservation Year (1970) of Epping Forest Conservation Centre at High Beech in the heart of the forest. The centre was built by the Corporation of London, which Parliament entrusted with the care of the 6,000 acres of Epping Forest as a public open space in 1878. Managed by the Field Studies Council, the centre's main work is to provide for the thousands of children who visit the forest in the course of their studies. In addition to this, the centre serves the public by arranging lectures, guided walks, less formal instruction for youth groups, and other activities. Operating in an area intended as a "lung for London", the Epping Forest Conservation Centre has already encountered the problem of vandalism, perpetrated in some instances by badly led groups.

At Hatfield Forest in Essex (not to be confused with Hatfield in Hertfordshire), the National Trust has launched an interesting experiment in an effort to solve the problem of caring for nature in a large public open space. Here, in this 1,000 acre stretch of woodland, with its open grassy rides and lake, about nine acres of marshland have been fenced and designated as a nature reserve. Managed by the Essex Naturalists' Trust whose voluntary workers undertake such tasks as the removal of hawthorn scrub, this small reserve is the haunt of snipe and ringed snakes and the habitat of marsh and spotted orchids – to mention but a few of the species present. Not that the remaining parts of Hatfield Forest are without interest for naturalists.

Similar praiseworthy co-operation is taking place in Essex at three other National Trust properties and, as a result, the Essex Naturalists' Trust is managing nature reserves at the Backwarden section of Danbury Common, an area favoured by nightingales, the 83½-acre Blakes Wood at Little Baddow, and Ray Island, an unspoilt salting in the Colne Estuary Site of Special Scientific Interest.

The Essex Naturalists' Trust is comparatively young, having been founded as recently as 1959 (the first county conservation trust, the Norfolk Naturalists' Trust, dates from 1926). Nevertheless it has become the largest County or Regional Trust in the country and one that has shown considerable enterprise. Its activities are centred on the splendid administrative and interpretative centre at Fingringhoe Wick, the Trust's nature reserve on the west bank of the Colne estuary, only four miles from Colchester. There is a public nature trail here, but the main part of this area of disused gravel workings and saltings is open to Trust members only.

The honorary wardens and assistant wardens of its nature reserves are a vital element in the Trust's organisation. One cannot praise them too highly, and one must never under-estimate the great importance of these dedicated volunteers as links between the trust and its supporters and those members of the general public who live, work or spend their leisure in the neighbourhood of the reserves in their care. There is space in this chapter to mention only a few of the trust's reserves (which number thirty-six at the time of writing), but its *Reserves Guide* gives full particulars, together with access and general information.

On the coast Colne Point Nature Reserve is a particularly important site. Here, on the east side of the Colne estuary, a shingle ridge over two miles long encloses some 400 acres of saltings, forming an area where some 200 species of birds have been identified. Wardening during the breeding season reduces human disturbance of nesting little terns, ringed plovers and other birds, but weather conditions and predators such as foxes can play havoc with such species, their eggs and chicks. Colne Point is also the habitat of a number of interesting plants, species ousted on so many parts of the coast by seaside development.

On a recent visit I was pleased to note that sea holly, with its spiny heads of attractive bluish flowers, survived there. A few days earlier while visiting All Saints' Church, Colchester, I was reminded of another activity which led to the virtual exter-mination of this plant on the Essex coast between the sixteenth and nineteenth centuries. On the wall of this ancient building, now the natural history museum, was a memorial to Samuel Great, member of the Dutch immigrant family De Groot (later Great), who died in 1706 aged eighty. Below this was exhibited a sample of candied sea holly root, Eringo root (as it was known), sold by him and other Colchester apothecaries as a medicine for complaints as various as consumption (tuber-culosis) and "obstructions of the urine, liver and gallbladder".

Colne Point was purchased in 1968 after the shingle ridges had ceased to be used for gravel extraction. A rather different story can be told of the Naze, a promontory stretching north-

wards from Walton-on-the-Naze, where the Essex Naturalists' Trust administers a twenty-acre nature reserve. In danger
of being 'developed' in the late 1950s – a threat averted by
opposition mobilized by the Essex Naturalists' Trust and other
local organizations – it became in the early 1960s a public open
space. Now one can walk over some 160 acres close to cliffs
noted for their classic exposure of the Red Crag, ancient
fossil-bearing deposits of sand and silt. Here, on this important
landfall for migrant birds, large gorse bushes provide shelter
and colour in due season. (Strictly speaking, there is no such
time, for, as every botanist knows: "When gorse is not in
bloom, kissing's out of season"). Down by the new sea wall are
lagoons, flooded at high tides, where one finds such salt-marsh
plants as sea aster, sea lavender and rice grass, and where dunlin
and redshank feed in the mud.

Moving towards the north-west of the county, one finds the
Essex Naturalists' Trust safeguarding two mixed deciduous
woods, Shadwell Wood, Ashdon, and West Wood, Little
Sampford, where the oxlip flourishes on soils of chalky boulder
clay. An attractive plant, this true oxlip bears deep yellow
primrose-like flowers in the many-flowered umbels of the
cowslip. Confined in Britain mainly to the area where
Cambridgeshire, Essex and Suffolk meet, it is still often mis-
taken for the primrose-cowslip hybrid, the so-called false oxlip,
a much commoner and more widespread plant.

Several Essex botanists were at the very centre of the
controversy that surrounded the oxlip during the last century
and well into the present one. One of them, Henry Doubleday
of Epping, discovered the true oxlip at Great Bardfield (hence
its old name Bardfield oxlip), grew it from seed, and sent
specimens to the Gardeners' Chronicle in order to prove that this
distinct species did grow in Britain.

In the extreme south of the county the Essex Naturalists'
Trust holds under licence from the Associated Portland
Cement Company fifty acres of disused chalk pit. A Site of
Special Scientific Interest, to which entry is limited to a few
named members concerned with management and recording,
this reserve is noted for its important 'chalk flora'. It is the only
Essex station of the man orchid, a rare plant whose survival
there appeared to be threatened at one time by the dumping of

chalk waste. The strawberry tree, a species often grown in gardens, thrives there, too, possibly as the result of seeds having been introduced by birds. Among the birds of this reserve is the kestrel.

This bird was adopted as the symbol of the Essex Naturalists' Trust whose motto "Watch over Essex" reminds us that it also acts as watchdog, seeking out and challenging threats to the county's wildlife.

The trust together with many individuals and organizations such as the Defenders of Essex Association successfully fought proposals to build a third London airport on the Maplin Sands off Foulness. It has since had to concentrate on opposing plans for a proposed Maplin Seaport, a complex of 2,500 acres which would extend offshore and bisect the Maplin Sands. Officially designated by the Nature Conservancy Council as a Site of Special Scientific Interest, this area of international ornithological importance lies outside the sea wall of Foulness, the island whose name, derived from the Old English *fugla-naess*, or 'wild birds' ness', means the promontory of wild birds.

Countless dunlin, knot, curlew, oystercatchers and other waders feed on small creatures that live in the vast sandflats. Thousands of dark-bellied brent geese feed on eel grass between sandflats and saltings, making this their main early winter feeding ground in Britain and probably the most important site in the world for the species. And one of the largest British breeding colonies of little terns lives on the huge banks of cockleshells at the north-east corner of Foulness. What will become of the island and its surroundings remains to be seen. Suffice it to say that thirteen conservation and other bodies have prepared a plan for public enjoyment of its landscape and wild life. This window on the wilderness would, it is suggested, include landward reserves run by voluntary conservation bodies and a seaward reserve of National Nature Reserve status managed by the Nature Conservancy Council. This responsible statutory body has already declared as a National Nature Reserve the twenty-acre Hales Wood near Saffron Walden, an oak-ash wood on chalky boulder clay, another habitat of oxlips. Parts of Two Tree Island, its adjoining saltmarshes and a large area of mudflats became Leigh National Nature Reserve when Southend-on-Sea Council rejected proposed commercial development and leased the land to the Nature Conservancy Council. The reserve includes some of the best surviving examples of saltmarshes in the Thames estuary, and its mudflats are a good feeding ground for dark-bellied brent geese.

Several local authorities in Essex are taking an active part in the nature conservation movement. One aspect of the interest shown by Southend-on-Sea Council has just been referred to, but earlier they established their own local nature reserve at Belfairs Wood whose trees include oaks, birches and horn-beams. The Naze, mentioned earlier, became a public open space when Essex County Council and the then Frinton and Walton Urban District Council bought the area. Harlow District Council has dedicated Great Parndon Wood as a local nature reserve, while Woodham Ferrers Parish Council allows Basildon Natural History Society to manage Woodham Fen, a haunt of reed buntings, meadow pipits and sandpipers at the tidal limit of two creeks running up from the River Crouch.

A particularly exciting moment in the history of nature conservation in Essex was when the Redundant Churches Fund offered the Essex Naturalists' Trust the use of Chickney churchyard, a grassy area near Broxted. The natural habitat of sweet violets, cowslips, goldilocks (a golden-yellow-flowered member of the buttercup family) and other species, it is likely to become a haven for rare Essex wild flowers. Already several young plants of sickle-leaved hare's-ear, a perennial herb with hollow stems and yellow flowers, have been planted there. Still regarded by some authorities as doubtfully native to this country, the plant had survived at Norton Heath, then its only British station, until 1962 when the removal of hedgerows, ditch cleaning, the re-alignment of telegraph poles, and fire all combined to destroy it. Fortunately Stanley Jermyn, who also gave seeds to the Royal Botanic Garden at Kew and to Cambridge University Botanic Garden, had grown the rare hare's-ear from seed. It was from his stock that plants were introduced to Fingringhoe Wick Nature Reserve, Sawbridgeworth Marsh Nature Reserve and, most recently, Chickney churchyard.

Another species which may well be included in this church-yard nature reserve is the Fyfield pea, a crimson-flowered scrambling perennial, whose name commemorates its original British station at Fyfield in Essex, a name much easier on the ear than that used in modern floras – earth-nut pea! Naturalized there in cornfields and hedges since about 1800, this attractive plant had become very scarce at Fyfield by the early 1970s when tubers were removed for cultivation in places of safety. Again the initiative came from Stanley Jermyn (and there are people who believe that there is now no field of activity where individuals can make really effective contributions!).

All this talk of councils and societies and of nature reserves of varying status must not be allowed to obscure the fact that many an Essex gardener assists the conservation of useful, attractive or otherwise interesting birds, insects and other creatures. Often a garden is small, but still large enough to contain a shrub whose berries attract hungry birds, even those irregular winter visitors waxwings. On occasion it is neglected, annoying tidier neighbours but providing thistle seeds for goldfinches or fallen apples for blackbirds and thrushes. As in so many other situations that arise in life, it is all a question of giving and taking, of gaining on the swings what you lose on the roundabouts. Thus – to turn to insects – a small patch of stinging nettles in a 'wild' corner of a garden might provide food for the larvae of small · tortoiseshell, peacock and red admiral butterflies whose beautiful winged forms will feed on nectar from flowers of such cultivated plants as Japanese stonecrop and 'Buddleia' (butterfly bush).

The decline of the peacock butterfly in parts of Essex has been attributed to the spraying of nettles, its main foodplant, notably on roadside verges. Spraying, cutting and other operations on roadside verges are also affecting a number of rare and beautiful wild plants. Bee orchids were cut down on one verge in north-west Essex despite the fact that it had been scheduled by the Essex Naturalists' Trust and notified to the county highways authority for special treatment. But such incidents should be avoided as co-operation develops between the trust and the authority and as more people help to list verges whose flora makes them suitable for special treatment. Formerly one rarely thought of these roadside verges without their associated hedgerows, but now one is forced to accept the fact that many of these shrubby protective barriers have been destroyed in recent years. Besides changing the appearance of parts of the county, this must affect the wild life in many ways. For example, the removal of bushes of the hawthorn, a plant commonly used for hedges, is taking from the landscape a shrub whose leaves, flowers and fruit are, in their own individual ways, attractive and colourful. At the same time, it is reducing not only the shelter available for birds and other creatures in a particular area, but also their potential food resources there.

Gone are the hawthorn leaves eaten by larvae of numerous moths (over a hundred species feed on hawthorn) and other insects. Gone are the hawthorn flowers whose attractiveness to bees, hover flies and beetles of many kinds is well-known. Gone, too, are the colourful fruit – the haws, food of species as varied as song thrushes and grey squirrels. The removal of other hedgerow shrubs (not to mention trees, climbers and scramblers) causes similar results, for there is hardly a plant whose presence, foliage, flowers and fruit do not affect some other living thing in some way.

The possible results of destroying plants, whether large or small, are not always taken seriously. But in recent years Essex naturalists have been concerned over the loss of many traditional sites of the white-letter hairstreak butterfly as the result of the high incidence of Dutch elm disease, killer of many thousands of this local insect's foodplants, elm and wych elm. Caused by a fungus, which is carried from elm to elm by two species of elm-bark beetles whose young adults mature on live elm bark but breed on dead and dying material, the disease is likely to discourage many people from planting elms. This is a sad prospect because they have long formed an integrated feature of many parts of the county landscape, and what is reputed to be the biggest smooth-leaved elm in the world survives at Saling in the Essex countryside.

In Essex much woodland including elms and other broad-leaved trees has been replanted with conifers. These pines, larches and other cone-bearing trees are not always viewed with approval, especially when grown massed together in tight formations to encourage the production of straight timber. Nevertheless certain of the 'alien' conifers have done very well in the county and are not without interest. At Lexden Manor, Colchester, a specimen of the monkey-puzzle (also called Chile pine), a South American species introduced to Britain in 1795, had grown to such a height that it was included by the Forestry Commission in a list of the oldest and largest specimens in this country. And Essex was among the first counties to cultivate the dawn redwood (or Chinese water-fir) when, only a year after its introduction to Britain, it was planted at Engelmann's nursery, Saffron Walden, in 1949. This attractive tree, the sole living species of a group long known from fossils, was found surviving in central China as recently as 1941.

Many of the broad-leaved trees of Essex were themselves originally introduced into the county, though some have long since become well established. The Lombardy poplar, its narrow spindle-shaped outline forming what that great tree-lover Miles Hadfield so aptly called "a notable exclamation mark in our scenery", lends a fresh touch to many parts of Essex and acts as the host-plant of aphids whose galls appear as curious growths on the leaves. Although it is often said to have been first brought to England from Turin by the Earl of Rochford and planted at his Essex home, St Osyth's Priory, in 1758, suggestions have recently been made that this elegant tree may well have been originally introduced by Archibald, Duke of Argyle who died in 1761.

Visitors to Chelmsford Cathedral are often puzzled by the curious truncated forms of the members of an avenue of locust trees whose scientific name *Robinia* commemorates Jean Robin, the French herbalist who brought the species to Europe from North America in 1601. Cobbett, who is best remembered as the author of *Rural Rides,* thought highly of this species, but very little came of his hopes for it, largely because the strong durable timber is so often contained in such twisted and deeply fluted trunks and branches.

Another introduced tree species, the horse chestnut, produces wood that is commercially useless. But few are not moved by the beauty of its large imposing flowers, and few would deny youngsters the pleasure derived from bashing the stringed nuts against one another in games of conkers (conquerors to serious students!). This 'foreigner' from Greece has done well in several parts of Essex, there being some particularly tall specimens between Forest Lodge and the lake in Hatfield Forest. These trees are survivors of ornamental planting carried out when the forest was in private ownership.

There are many such relics in Essex and those with patience and persistence will discover that people and events associated with them are often every bit as interesting as the wild creatures that live on and about them. Imagine, for example, what fascinating facts make up the history of the great Tasmanian cider gum trees at Brightlingsea. What induced John Bateman of Brightlingsea Hall Farm who, in 1887, received seed of this eucalyptus (for that is what it is) to make what Elwes and Henry – those great authorities on trees – regarded as the most remarkable plantation of this species in England?

Numerous smaller introduced plants also occur here and Jermyn's *Flora of Essex* mentions many of them, including several species of stonecrop, American willow-herb, evening primrose, Persian ivy, and giant hogweed – to mention but a few. One of them, the hispid perennial herb Russian comfrey, is worthy of special note, for it was at Coggeshall in Essex that many of the early experiments into the value of this fast-growing, high-yielding fodder plant were carried out by Henry Doubleday, Quaker smallholder and cousin of the Epping entomologist of the same name, who had imported it from Russia in the early 1870s. Despite Henry Doubleday's claim that the crop produced a good yield of fodder when cut four or five times a season and that it lasted twenty years if the land was kept clean and occasionally stirred, comfrey growing declined. Odd plants survived on hedgebanks and roadsides and then, in 1900, Webster's nurseries of Stock, Essex, imported fresh supplies of comfrey from Russia and continued to sell it for some sixty years. One of their customers was Lawrence D. Hills, author of standard works on the crop, to whom I am greatly indebted for information.

After failing to find a house at Coggeshall, where Doubleday had died in 1902, Hills moved to Bocking in 1954 and there established the Henry Doubleday Research Association. His trial ground was planted with comfrey, samples coming from growers in various parts of the country and from hedgerows surrounding land at Coggeshall where Henry Doubleday had been active more than fifty years before. Now the Association, with over 4,000 members from all parts of the world, not only undertakes research into all aspects of Russian comfrey, including concentrating it for protein-rich human food, but also into improved methods of organic farming and gardening, the control of plant pests and disease without persistent chemicals, and several related matters.

The introduced animals of Essex include the grey squirrel, a North American species which seems to be just as much at home in town gardens as in such areas of woodland as Hatfield Forest. About 1910, before grey squirrels appeared there, red squirrels, said to have been examples of the continental race bought in Leadenhall Market, were successfully introduced into Epping Forest by a local landowner who thought that the native red squirrels were dying out. North American mink, rapacious carnivores originating from fur farms, have caused some trouble in Essex but quick and effective action is normally taken against this serious pest. The small muntjac or barking deer, natives of Asia whose escape from Woburn Park, Bedfordshire, in the last century allowed them to spread through several counties, occur in dense vegetation at Hatfield, Epping, Honey Wood (Halstead), and Walden (east and west of Saffron Walden) Forests.

For the interest and convenience of people who lack the time or do not feel disposed to track down these and other animals in the wild, there are a number of good collections of living animals in the county. At their best such collections offer visitors the chance of being both entertained and educated, at the same time creating through breeding successes stocks of animals for transfer to other collections and, in certain special cases, protected areas in the wild.

Muntjac, just mentioned, are among several species of deer kept at Mole Hall Wildlife Park at Widdington, near Newport. This collection of mammals and birds was started by the director, Mrs Pamela Johnstone, and her husband in 1948 and first opened to the public in 1964. It is in the grounds of their home, an ancient moated house first mentioned as 'Molehalle' in 1286 in the *Registrum Evidentarium* of Takeley Priory. Many species have bred in the Mole Hall collection, which received the Gavin Maxwell Award for breeding Canadian otters and an additional award for the fact that they were third generation captivity born. Another achievement was successful breeding from a pair of servals whose two kittens were hand-reared from the age of eight days owing to the ineptitude of the mother. Other mammals bred include four species of deer, Bennett's wallaby, capuchins, North American raccoon and coatimundi. Birds, too, are well represented in the Mole Hall Wildlife Park where green winged, blue and gold, and scarlet macaws from South America add colour to the collection and where several kinds of ducks and geese are seen swimming in the moat. In one year alone five clutches of black swan cygnets were reared from one pair of adults, while in 1975 some Rothschild's mynahs were bred but unfortunately they did not survive. Among the many other birds that have bred at Mole Hall are the Sarus crane, a native of India, and the nene or Hawaiian goose, a sedentary species of the islands of Hawaii and Maui whose propagation in captivity has not only greatly increased the population, which was down to thirtyfive in 1950, but has also resulted in many birds being released in the wild again.

Mole Hall tends to specialise in the smaller mammals, but the collection at Colchester Zoo includes many of the larger species, including elephants, giraffes and representatives of the big cats. Housed in the grounds of Stanway Hall, about three miles from the town centre, this zoo, with its lawns and picnic areas, amusement arcade and model railway, is a popular spot for family outings. Tigers, black panthers, lions, lemurs and llamas are among the species bred there, all surplus stock going to other zoos in Britain.

An event that caused much interest was the birth in 1971 (followed by another in 1973) of a 'zedonk', a hybrid or cross-breed with a zebra as its sire and a black Arabian ass as its dam. Two species whose numbers have been severely reduced in the wild, the American bison and the white rhinoceros, are also represented at Colchester where one hopes they will eventually be bred. The many birds in the collection include elegant pink flamingoes and large colourful macaws, whose aviary was being visited by a flock of hungry wild greenfinches during my last visit to the zoo. But what to many people must be one of the most fascinating exhibits is the collection of different species of owls of various sizes, which is imaginatively housed in and around the ruins of the church of All Saints whose late-fourteenth-century tower is of bands of flint and brick.

A zoo and ecology centre form part of the large family recreation centre at Basildon. The zoo has lions, leopards and pumas, which have all produced litters, and also monkeys and a large variety of birds, while the ecology centre houses birds, reptiles, fish and other animals. There is also a small zoo at Vange, now included in Basildon New Town designated area, where Dama wallabies, pumas and various birds have bred.

What is definitely not a zoo, though it is open to the public on a limited number of days outside the breeding season, is Daw's Hall Wildfowl Farm at Lamarsh in the Stour valley, not far from the Essex-Suffolk border. The owner, Major Iain Grahame, specialises in breeding rare and endangered breeds of waterfowl and pheasants, and has built up one of the most successful breeding establishments for these birds in the world. He describes in his book *Blood pheasant, a Himalayan adventure* how, in 1970, he went to the Himalayas to collect live specimens of the blood pheasant, a rather small species resembling a partridge in shape and the one breed of pheasant that had not then been successfully kept or bred in captivity. Breeding success was achieved in 1971, young being hatched and reared at the Wildfowl Farm at Lamarsh, and again in three of the following four years, the original pair having survived. Such results with a species whose various subspecies live at high altitudes in the Himalayas and on the mountains of western and northern China show that, as in so many other fields of activity, dedication and determination are vital elements in nature conservation.

Appropriately Major Grahame, who was Chairman of the Essex Supporters Group of the World Wildlife Fund for many years, has been appointed Secretary of the World Pheasant Association, a newly-formed international charitable organization devoted to the conservation of all 240 members of the order Galliformes (pheasants and such related birds as megapodes, curassows, grouse, partridges, guineafowl and wild turkeys) with initial emphasis on the pheasant family on account of the severe position of most species in the wild. Only a few months after its formation, the World Pheasant Association indicated that it wanted action and, what is most important, action that involved individuals, members who were prepared to participate in the project of sending eggs laid in Britain to India and Pakistan being invited to lend breeding pairs or trios of monal, cheer and white-crested kalij pheasants. True lovers of nature will surely applaud such action, those living in Essex recognizing with added satisfaction that projects promoted by a body based in their county may well save from extermination a most important group of birds.

This chapter began with references to common organisms and ends with talk of certain rare and endangered species. There is no contradiction here: the true lover of nature is concerned with both rare and common species, with plants and creatures that cannot really be called beautiful as well as those displaying great beauty. Let us hope that more and more Essex people will care for nature and that they and their children will enjoy the fruits of their efforts.

X

CULTURAL AND LEISURE ACTIVITIES

ESSEX is very fortunate in having within its boundaries local authorities, organizations and individuals who devote themselves wholeheartedly to the provision of facilities for the pursuit of cultural and other leisure activities. Opportunities created in this way are without question invaluable in an age when many people gain little, if any, real satisfaction from their daily work. They enable those who so desire to fill some at least of their off-duty hours with activities affording a sense of genuine personal interest, active participation, or individual achievement. For many workers in the complex hierarchies of modern bureaucracy and business, where computers are often treated with far more consideration than people, their leisure provides chances of developing balanced individuality, initiative, enterprise, responsibility and stable personality. To a free nation these are vital factors whose importance is so often ignored. Essex must surely continue its policy of actively encouraging their growth.

It will come as no surprise to readers who have followed me through the earlier chapters of this book, with their many references to people and places of historical interest, that there are in Essex a number of organizations actively concerned with various aspects of the county's past. The Friends of Historic Essex, a society founded in 1954, assists the County Council Committee controlling the Essex Record Office by contributing towards the cost of publications and indexes and of certain objects at Ingatestone Hall where exhibitions are held from April to October. Members enjoy social activities, including meetings, music recitals and visits to historic houses not open to the public. Based at County Hall, Chelmsford, where original documents, now over two million in number, have been housed since 1938, the Essex Record Office has a branch dealing mainly with records relating to south-east Essex at Southend-on-Sea public library.

The old-established Essex Archaeological Society is another vital force. Besides publishing its *Transactions,* an invaluable source of information to members and others, it is always ready with advice and assistance. An example of the Society's readiness to cooperate with others occurred when it worked with Essex County Council archaeologists during a 'dig' at a site awaiting development in Saffron Walden. Here interesting details of the town's growth resulted from the discovery of the defence ditch forming part of the outer bailey of the Norman castle.

There are many historical and archaeological societies connected with particular towns or parts of the country, details of which may often be obtained from local reference libraries and newspapers. Most of them cater not only for people whose interest is well established but also for 'beginners'. Their programmes include talks and visits to places of interest, and a few, such as Waltham Abbey Historical Society, have museums housing local history and archaeological exhibits.

Experts have often urged local historians to arm themselves with appropriate Ordnance Survey maps and take to the countryside on foot in search of the evidence of history. Happily there are in Essex many active groups of the Ramblers' Association, Holiday Fellowship and other bodies. They may not always be especially interested in historical or archaeological matters, but they afford opportunities of companionship and of taking part in rambles throughout the year. The fact that some thirty-eight rambles in various parts of Essex were listed for a recent month is an indication of the great interest in this form of activity. There are in Essex numerous public rights of way and two long-distance footpath routes, Essex Way from Epping to Dedham and Forest Way from Epping Forest to Hatfield Forest, have been marked out.

A study of the people associated with the county's history reveals that over the years many Essex folk have been actively involved in the world of music. This great tradition continues to this day. So many towns and villages have choirs, choral societies and music clubs that it is not possible to list them all here. Harlow has its Organ Club, Chelmsford its Opera Group, and south-east Essex its Hammond Organ Society, while Basildon has an Amateur Operatic Society (shortly to celebrate its 50th anniversary) and YOBA, Youth Opera Basildon Area, whose members have taken part in La Bohème, Orpheus in the Underworld, and other productions. The encouragement of young people is a very pleasing aspect of musical life in the county. Essex Youth Orchestra gives its members valuable experience and training and the public in Essex, London and other parts of the world considerable pleasure. What a wonderful idea that the profits from Thaxted's pageant of 500 years of dance, drama, music and song should go to Essex Youth Orchestra whose members often perform in the church there.

Those who derive interest and aesthetic pleasure from paintings, sculpture and other works of art are just as well provided for in Essex. Facilities for art exhibitions and allied activities are indeed growing all the time. With the restoration by Essex County Council of its old Corn Exchange, Saffron Walden now has a Library and Arts Centre where it is possible to present exhibitions, simple theatre, concerts, recitals and social events for local cultural organizations. There are other centres at Little Baddow Hall and at the Old House, Shenfield, home of Brentwood Art Society, and, as the reader will have discovered from an earlier chapter, Basildon and Harlow have excellent facilities, too.

One gains a vivid impression of the artistic endeavours of both professionals and amateurs by visiting exhibitions in various parts of the county. Thus towards the end of the year one finds members of the Colchester Art Society showing works of all types (152 works in 1976) in the splendid surroundings of The Minories at Colchester. As members of organizations known variously as societies, clubs and groups, artists in Braintree, Brentwood, Great Bentley, Frinton, Saffron Walden, and many other places bring their work to the attention of the public who, even if they do not make a purchase, rarely remain completely unmoved by some at least of the results of creative work.

The art of the photographer, whose contribution complements that of the artist working in paint, pencil and other media, is represented in Essex in exhibitions organized by photographic and camera clubs. Colchester Camera Club, for example, has brought together an impressive collection of pictures of the town that made its title, "Towns are more than bricks and mortar", ring true. Apart from their creation of valuable archive material and objects of beauty (for well produced photographs and slides can be all this and more), Essex photographers evidently generate much friendship, in itself a valuable activity. Their print and slide 'battles', when teams and clubs compete with one another, do not harm anyone, though they may on occasion deflate the self-important, which is not a bad thing!

The amateur theatre is another form of art in which many people find satisfaction and enjoyment. Fortunately Essex has its amateur dramatic societies and other groups of players whose appearances take place in settings as varied as Harlow Playhouse and Tiptree Factory Hall, Blackmore Village Hall and the Jubilee Hall at Maldon, the University of Essex Theatre at Wivenhoe and Basildon Arts Centre Theatre.

Poetry readings are also held at a number of these places, a fact which will not surprise those who appreciate the extent of the support there is in Essex for this vital form of expression of thought and feeling. The magazine *Poetry Essex* publishes the work of Essex writers, the Essex Poets Group acts as what has been called a 'performing group', and Frederic Vanson's column 'Poetry in Essex' is a regular source of news in the monthly magazine *Essex Countryside*, all helping to stimulate and develop interest. The Friends of Essex Poets (FEP) is a lively body, the envy of poets in many another county. A recent FEP open competition attracted over 300 entries from Essex and a grant from Harlow Arts Council to cover the cost of an anthology of the prize-winning poems, and a one-day poetry school and festival was a great success.

The growing list of published Essex poets includes such names as Stanley J. Thomas, whose recent work includes the collection *November Man*, Frederic Vanson *(Seeing and other Poems* and at least six other collections) Tully Potter (read his collection *The Emigrant*), Edward Boaden Thomas *(Twelve Parts of Derbyshire)*, Pam Croome *(House of Cards)*, and Marguerite Wood, whose *Crack Me the Shell* contains twenty-four poems.

Most genuine poets have much in common with true

nature-lovers and, as we have seen, Essex has bred and nurtured many of each. Earlier I sang the praises of some of the county's naturalists. I have already written, too, of a few of the natural history organizations of Essex, but one must not forget the others, each important in its own way, each waiting to welcome and encourage new members. Long an active body, the Essex Field Club is involved in a wide range of natural history and allied interests. Its events include 'bottle hunts', the search for mammalian remains in discarded bottles, an annual British wildlife photographic competition, lectures on such topics as Essex archaeological excavations, the wildlife of the county and also that of distant places, and rambles. The local societies include Basildon, Colchester, South Essex, Thurrock, and Witham Natural History Societies, Epping Forest Branch of the British Naturalists' Association, Harlow and District Wildlife Society, and St Osyth Bird-watching and Protection Club.

Closely related to these natural history organizations are the various horticultural and gardening bodies. Well established in most parts of Essex, they arrange talks, demonstrations and shows. The shows, often held on a seasonal basis in spring, summer and autumn, afford members opportunities of displaying the results of their labours of love. They attract public attention, too, and often lead to the recruitment of new members and the fostering of a wider interest in plants, crops and gardens. In the wide and friendly world of plants and plantsmen there is room for everyone. The Essex zone of the National Cactus and Succulent Society has its annual zone show and prizes are certainly not confined to people with large gardens or expensive greenhouses. Chelmsford Chrysanthemum and Dahlia Society runs its own show, attracting growers and admirers of these splendid plants with flowers of so many forms and colours. There are local groups in Essex of several national specialist societies, too. The Alpine Garden Society has two, Essex and Epping Forest groups, and it is pleasing to find Essex alpine gardeners among the officers and committee members of the parent body.

Like those gardeners who concentrate on growing flowers, the county's Flower and Floral Decoration Clubs do a lot to bring colour and beauty into our lives. Their interest is shared by members of the Women's Institutes who also concern themselves with cookery, house and garden matters, drama, photography, problems of contemporary life in town and country, tennis and bowls, and every conceivable form of handicrafts. In a county with more than 300 Women's Institutes and some 18,000 members, the movement exerts a considerable social and educational influence. In Essex this is by no means confined to women, for the County Federation has made great efforts to involve the whole family in, for example, their house and garden two-day event, with its competitions, entertainments, displays and stalls, and husbands have been invited to conferences on Europe. Elsewhere there was a case of two husbands, disguised as village ancients, demanding admittance to a WI meeting under the Sex Discrimination Act!

In Essex husbands are also welcomed by the Townswomen's Guilds to variety shows and certain other social functions. But these are only a few of the activities of a movement whose golden jubilee occurs in 1978. Art exhibitions, flower shows, musical days, talks and conferences are arranged, while at the international level there are exchange visits with women in such other countries as Denmark and Germany. Charities benefit from some events and often gifts are made to individuals, a knitted blanket to an old person, a doll's house to an orphan, and so on. There has been some concern that the Guilds, whose membership includes many housewives, should be more involved with current problems. Certainly they have much to contribute and their representation at, for instance, a conference on 'Violence in the community' was well worthwhile.

Violence and vandalism, seen as the result of causes as varied as boredom, social pressures and resentment, are often thought to be counteracted by *active* enjoyment of leisure facilities, particularly outdoor ones. Be this as it may, there is no question of Essex lacking opportunities for such involvement by people of all ages. The county, an important yachting centre with fine sailing waters, has provided, on the southern side of the Blackwater estuary, a Field Studies and Sailing Centre offering sailing and canoeing instruction and facilities for boatbuilding and field-study courses. Elsewhere along the coast and estuaries yachting and sailing clubs, including several well-known ones, are open to those with the necessary ability and experience.

Fishing is enjoyed in Essex by large numbers of people, young and old alike, many of the county's rivers, reservoirs and coastal waters offering good sport. Sea-angling clubs are active at Harwich, Walton-on-the-Naze, Clacton-on-Sea, and Canvey Island. There is sea-fishing from the piers at Harwich, Walton, Clacton and Southend, from the shore at various points along the coast, and also from offshore boats. The many varieties of fish to be caught include cod, bass, whiting, dogfish, and mullet. Freshwater fishing is available in the upper reaches of a number of Essex rivers and also at such other places as the lake in Hatfield Forest (three miles east of Bishop's Stortford), where pike, tench, roach, rudd and perch occur, and Gosfield lake, near Halstead. Essex attracts fishermen from other parts of the country, but one of the county's own anglers, Mr Gordon Farrell of Thundersley, won the 1975 National Shore Fishing Championship (and the Winfield Sportsman trophy) when he visited the Teign estuary to take part in the finals of this event.

Given suitable weather, swimming can be enjoyed along the Essex coast for several months of the year, but indoor pools, now widespread in the county, obviously make this healthy activity possible at all times. Less dependent on the weather, riding is another enjoyable pursuit that is taken up by Essex folk of all ages. There are places along the coast where riders may take to the sands. The Southend-on-Sea area is particularly well provided with riding schools and there is a trotting track at Belfairs Woods, a favourite place of local riders. Inland Epping Forest is very popular with riders and there are several riding schools in the district. Riding to hounds continues to appeal to people from both rural and urban backgrounds and Essex is one of those counties where a number of hunts are still active. The Essex has its kennels at Old Harlow, while those of the East Essex and the Essex Union are at Earls Colne and Billericay respectively. Two other hunts bearing the county name are the Essex and Suffolk, with its kennels at Hadleigh in Suffolk, and the Essex Farmers'.

Hare-hunting on foot has its devotees in Essex. The Colchester Garrison Beagles, Mid-Essex Beagles, and the De

Burgh and North Essex Harehounds (an amalgamation of the
North Essex Foot Beagles and the De Burgh Basset hounds) are
active, the total number of hounds in these three packs being
fifty-one couple. There are people who object, often strongly,
to field sports, and their opinions must be respected. There are
others who, in the case of hare-hunting, enjoy the sight of
hounds twisting and turning with their quarry, and experience
a sense of satisfaction when the pack runs well and with a good
cry. They regard greyhound racing, with its mechanically
propelled hare and enclosed track, as a very poor substitute (if
indeed it can truthfully be called a substitute) for hare-hunting
in the open. All the same, greyhound racing has its followers in
Essex and Southend Stadium is one of Britain's best-known
meeting places for the sport.

Golf, affording players exercise in the fresh air, often in
beautiful surroundings, is popular in Essex. There are public
eighteen-hole courses at Belfairs Municipal course (near Leigh-
on-Sea), Brentwood, and elsewhere, while nine-hole and
eighteen-hole club courses are found throughout the county.
Equally widespread provision is made in Essex for those who
play tennis, public and club courts being available in most
places. Frinton-on-Sea is famous for its tennis tournaments, the
well-equipped club having twenty-two grass courts and four
hard courts. The Frinton tennis week is held each July and the
junior tournament in August.

As a cricketing county, Essex has its own county team based,
as we have seen, at Chelmsford. It was a most heartening
experience to hear that one of the principal aims of Essex
County Cricket Club, as it completed its centenary year, is to
encourage all those in the county, particularly young people,
who want, in some way, to participate in the game. This is a
most praiseworthy aim in a county which has produced some
great cricketers, grows fine cricket-bat willows, and is still the
scene of that most delightful activity of the English countryside
– cricket on the village green. Cricket was, of course, played
and enjoyed in Essex long before the County Club was formed.
According to John Crosier, an eighteenth-century miller and
farmer of Maldon, a transcript of whose diary is in Essex
Record Office, the gentlemen of Maldon "associated into a
cricket club" in 1786. Evidently some members were not

over-keen on the game, for they remained at the 'Ship', smoking their pipes and playing cards, while a 'regular set' played cricket. These regular players must have communicated their enthusiasm to other active cricketers. Certainly by 1800 the Maldon side were able to beat the Winstree Hundred Club "and 57 runs over".

Bowls, long part of the English scene, is a popular game throughout Essex, many towns and villages having well-kept greens. Each year, in July and August, Southend-on-Sea, a town well provided with municipal greens, many of Cumberland turf, is host to competitors in the men's and women's annual open bowling tournaments. Southend also holds an open hockey festival each Easter. Like the game itself in the county, this event is well supported. At Easter, too, Southend arranges an open festival for association football (and also one for the rather less popular Rugby football). Colchester United and Southend United, the county's top two football teams, compete in the Football League. Other Essex football teams play in the Southern, Athenian, Eastern Counties, Border, and Essex Senior Leagues. Football was one of several "rustic amusements" enjoyed at county fêtes during the nineteenth century. Another was archery, a sport that is still enjoyed in Essex, albeit by comparatively few people at present. Southend Archery Club meets regularly, as do Harlow Bowmen, and some of the county's multi-purpose sports centres provide facilities for this ancient sport.

Compared with others already mentioned, gliding is a comparatively new sport. In Essex, as in so many other places, it is, however, becoming increasingly popular. Essex Gliding Club operates from North Weald aerodrome, while Essex and Suffolk Gliding Club is based at Manningtree. Water skiing is enjoyed at places on the coast and also at Gosfield Lake, near Halstead, and several branches of the British Sub Aqua Club operate in the county.

Essex has not been content merely to enjoy such natural amenities as its fine sailing and fishing waters, but has provided facilities to compensate in some measure for its lack or shortage of certain others. There is, for example, at Harlow Sports Centre an artificial ski-slope, though one hastens to add that, in hard winters with deep snow covering the ground, people are not slow to try out their skis and toboggans on natural slopes in Harlow Town Park.

Those who planned Harlow made a point of retaining a number of the old country lanes. This was an excellent idea for these ancient thoroughfares throughout the town now serve as safe tracks for the use of horse riders and cyclists. Racing cyclists taking part in national events, as well as less competitive riders, find enjoyment here. Harlow Cycling Club is one of many such organizations in the county, Colchester Rovers and Chelmsford's Chelmer Cycling Club being especially well known.

Facilities for many sports and other leisure interests not already mentioned are provided in Essex at Sports Centres, stadia, athletics tracks, and other centres. Looking down the list for a single town one finds the names of clubs whose members are interested in athletics, badminton, basketball, bridge, camping, chess, dog training, homing pigeons, judo, netball, squash rackets, surfing, table tennis, and youth hostelling. There are undoubtedly Essex towns and villages which could, without difficulty, add to this list. Let us hope that there will always be so many indications of initiative, enterprise, and healthy, constructive activity in Essex, a county so much part of an England whose original greatness stemmed from these very qualities.

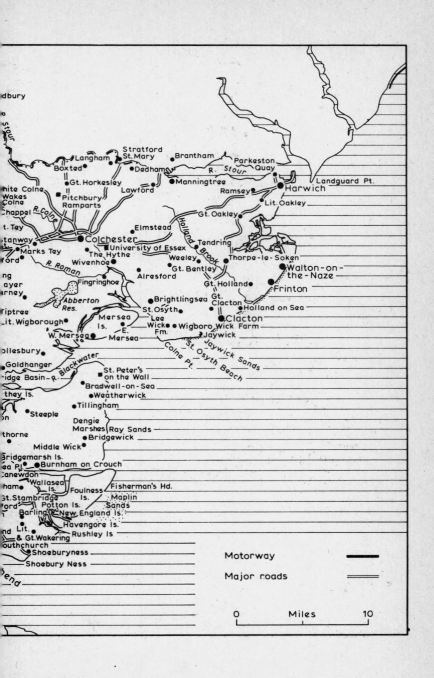

Motorway ▬▬▬

Major roads ══

0   Miles   10

INDEX

Abberton Reservoir, 52, 66
Abbess Roding, 63
Abdy family, 65
Abridge, 65
ACROW, 143
Agricultural Statistics England and Wales 1973,
  116
Agriculture, 30, 40, 43, 48, 89, 91, 116-33
Aircraft Museum, Historic, 46
Alberni String Quartet, 104
Albyns, 65
Alfalfa, 119
Alfred the Great, 22
Allen, Benjamin, 149
——, Dr Matthew, 96-7
Alresford, 53
Althorne, 60
Ambresbury Banks, 20
Amphibians, 153
Anchor Press, 152
Anne, Princess, 79
Aquatels, Basildon, 112
Aragon, Catherine of, 93
Archery, 175
Arden Hall, 91-2
Ardleigh, 19
Ardleigh Laminated Plastics, 136
Argyle, Archibald, Duke of, 161
Arts, the, 104-5, 111, 168-70
Arts Council of Great Britain, 111
Ascham, Roger, 65
Ashdon, 129, 156
Ashingdon, 23, 60
Associated Portland Cement Company, 156
Athelstan, King, 22
Audley, Lord, 87
——, Sir Thomas, 27, 76, 87
Audley End Mansion, 25, 87-8
Augustine, St, 21
Ayrshire cattle, 121
Aythorpe Roding, 63

Bacon, John, 69
Baddow Pippin, 125
Baker, W. J., 140
Balkerne Gate, 74
Ball, John, 26
Ball bearings, 139
Bardfield oxlip, 156
Barley, 118
Barling, 62
Barns, timber-framed, 17
Barrett family, 139
Barrington, Sir Francis, 27
Basildon, 55, 81, 107-15, 138, 141-2, 146-7,
  165
—— Amateur Operatic Society, 169
—— Development Corporation, 107, 109,
  113
—— District Council, 108
—— Golf Club, 112
—— Natural History Society, 113, 158, 171
—— Sports Council, 111-12
—— and District Arts Association, 111
Bata, Tomas, 138
Bateman, John, 162
Battails Hall, 67
Battle River, 59
Battlesbridge, 59
Battles Hall, 67
'Bays and Says', 77-8
Beaker peoples, 19
Beauchamp Roding, 64
Beche, John, 27, 76
Beckett, Reginald, 115
Beeleigh Abbey, 59
Belchamp St Paul, 17
Belfairs Municipal course, 174
Belfairs Wood, 158
Belfries, timber-framed, 15-16
Belgae, 19-20, 73
Benfleet, 22, 44, 136, 142, 150
Bentall, William, 142-3

Bernard & Sons Ltd, 138
Berners Roding, 64
Betjeman, Sir John, 86
Billericay, 31, 90-1, 138, 141, 145, 173
Birds, 150-1, 155-8, 164-6
Bishopsfield, Harlow, 100
Bishop's Stortford, 67
Blaber, Charles, 39
Black Death, 25-6
Black Notley, 148-9
Blackmore, 56
Blackwater, River, 41-2, 53-5, 59, 142
Blakes Wood, Little Baddow, 154
Blunt, A. J. G., 126-7
Boat-building, 136
Booking, 53-4, 85, 136-7, 162
Boggis, Isaac, 79
——, Thomas, 78-9
Bohun, Humphrey de, 84
Boleyn, Sir Thomas, 61
——, Anne, 61
Bonner, Edmund, 92
Book binding, 152
Booth, General, 47
Boreham, 89-90
Borstal, 86
Bosworth, Battle of, 26
Boudicca, 80, 88
Boulogne, Count Eustace of, 64
Bourchier family, 26
Bowls, 175
Boxted, 13
Brabazon of Tara, Lord, 42
Bradwell, 54
Bradwell-on-Sea, 14, 21, 42, 71
Brain, River, 54
Braintree, 28-9, 54, 137, 143-4, 148-9
Branch, David C., 110-11
Brantham, 52
Braybrooke, First Lord, 88
——, Seventh Lord, 88
Brendon, Wm & Son Ltd, 152
Brentwood, 28-30, 92-3, 128-9, 146-7, 174
Brentwood Art Society, 169
Brewing, 134-5
Brick, 13-15
Brick-making, 48, 135-6
Bridgemarsh Island, 60
Bridgewick, 43
Brightlingsea, 40-1, 50, 136, 162
Brightlingsea Yacht Club, 40
British Bata Shoe Company, 138-9
British Naturalists' Association, 171

British Sub-Aqua Club, 175
Britnoth, 53
Bronze Age, 19
Broomfield, 56, 125
Broomway, the, 43-4
Broomwood, Chignal, 150
Brown, A. F. J., 38
——, Ralph, 105
Browne, Sir Anthony, 92
Brummell, Beau, 53
Brussels, Steamship, 36
Buck, Frederick, 152
Budworth, Captain P. J., 95
Buildings of England, The, 15
Bulmer Brick and Tile Co., 136
Burgh, Hubert de, 46-7, 93
Burnham-on-Crouch, 61, 136
Burnham Sailing Club, 61
Bury St Edmunds, 94
Butler, Lord, 82
Butterflies and larger Moths of Essex, A Guide
to the, 151
Butyl Products, 145-6

Caesar, Julius, 19-20
Cam, River, 88
Camden, William, 33, 86
Campion, Edmund, 92
CAMRA, 135
Camulodunum, 20, 73
Can, River, 56-7
Canewdon, 60
Cants of Colchester, 128
Canvey Island, 28, 48-50, 138, 173
Capel family, 63
Caratacus, 20
Carreras Rothmans Ltd, 146
Castle Hedingham, 12, 14, 24-6, 52, 151
Castle House, Dedham, 135
Catamarans, 136
Cattle, 40
Catuvellauni, 19-20
Cedd, St, 21, 42, 71
Cement, 34, 136
Chancellor, Frederic, 61
Chantry House, Billericay, 90
Chappel, 53
Charles I, King, 27-8
—— II, King, 28-9, 88
Charlotte, Princess, 45
Charolais cattle, 121
Chartist Association, 94
Chatham, Lord, 36

Cheese-making, 39-40, 43, 116
Chelmer, River, 54-9, 69
Chelmer and Blackwater Navigation, 55, 57-9
Chelmer Cycling Club, 176
Chelmsford, Bishop of, 70-1
——, 16, 25, 28-30, 56-7, 69-72, 92, 121, 130-1, 133, 135, 139-42, 174, 176
—— Cathedral, 70-1, 161
——, excursions from, 83-97
—— *Chronicle: or, Essex Weekly Advertiser, the,* 72
—— Chrysanthemum and Dahlia Society, 171
—— Morris Side, 72
—— Opera Group, 168
—— Rugby Football Club, 71
—— Tool and Gauge Co, 139
—— *and Essex Weekly News, the,* 72
Chickney churchyard, 158
Chignal, 150
Chippinghill, Witham, 22, 89
Chipping Ongar, 56, 64
Chivelyng, William, 75
Chrishall, 13
Christianity, 21
Christy, Miller, 150
Cigarette manufacturing, 146
Civil wars, 27-8
Clactonian culture, 18
Clacton-on-Sea, 18, 29, 39, 127, 173
Clare, John, 96-7
Claudius, Emperor, 20, 73-4, 80
Clavering, 13, 24, 67
Clay, 13
Clement V, Pope, 17
Cloth trade, 27, 30, 77-9, 85, 89, 137-8
Clunch, 12
Cnut, 23, 60
Coast, 33-50
Coastal Radio Ltd, 141
Cobbett, William, 161
Coggeshall, Ralph de, 47
——, 25, 47, 54, 136, 153, 162
Colchester, 12-14, 16, 19-22, 24-30, 37, 39, 42, 53, 62, 72-82, 125, 128-9, 135, 138, 140, 144, 152, 155, 155, 161
—— Art Society, 169
—— Borough Council, 78
—— Camera Club, 169-70
—— Civic Society, 66
—— Garrison Beagles, 173-4
—— Natural History Society, 171

—— Rovers, 176
—— United,175
—— Zoo, 66, 164-5
—— and Essex Museum, 19-20, 24
Collister, E. R. and Associates, 110
Colne, River, 26, 40-1, 52-3, 66, 72-3, 82, 154-5
—— Point, 40, 155
Colt family, 68
Columbus, the English, 67
Comfrey, 162-3
Community Associations, 105-6
—— health care, 106
Concrete, Aerated, 136
Constable, Golding, 135
——, John, 46, 51, 82, 90, 135
Copford, 14, 66
Copperas, 34
Corn dollies, 54
Coryton, 145
Countryside Commission, 113
Courtaulds, 30, 52, 136-8
Crays Hill, 59
Creeksea, 60-1
Cressing, 17
Cricket, 71, 174-5
Cricket-bat willow, 130
Cricks Green, Felsted, 129
Cripsey Brook, 64
Crittall Windows Ltd, 143-4
Crompton, Colonel, 139
Cromwell, Oliver, 27
Croome, Pam, 170
Croppenburgh, Joas, 48
Crosier, John, 174-5
Crouch, River, 42-3, 59-62, 158
Crouch Yacht Club, 61
Crummy, Philip, 72
Cunobelin, 20, 73
Cunobelin, 20, 73
Cutlery industry, 86
Cutte, Sir John, 15
Cycling, 176
Cyclists, services for, 64

Danbury Common, 154
Danbury Hill, 57
Danes in Essex, 21-3, 60
D'Arcy Spice apple, 125
Dartmouth, Countess of, 86-7
Davey, Paxman & Co., 144
Daw's Hall Wildfowl Farm, 165-6
Debden, 55, 129

De Burgh and North Essex Harehounds, 173-4
Dedham, 51, 135-6, 168
Dedham Vale Society, 51
Defence, Ministry of, 43
Defenders of Essex Association, 157
De Groot family, 155
Dengie peninsula, 42-3
Devall, Peter, 79
Devereux, Robert, 63
Dissenters, 29
Dissolution, the, 26-7, 61-2, 68, 87
Distilling, 135
Domesday Book, 24, 85, 129
Donyland Wood, 66
Doubleday, Edward, 152
——, Henry (Coggeshall), 162-3
——, Henry (Epping), 152, 156
Dovercourt, 28, 36, 152
Driffield, Rev. Walter Wren, 90
Duck-decoy ponds, 43
Dunmow Flitch Bacon Company, 123
Dunstan, St, 22
Dutch Quarter, Colchester, 78
—— elm disease, 160
—— wars, 28
Dyer family, 85

Earls Colne, 25, 53, 90, 143, 173
East Essex Hunt, 173
East Mersea, 41
East Saxons, 21, 42
East Tilbury, 28, 138-9
Eastern Association, 27
Eastwood, 46
Edgar the Peaceable, 22
Edmund, King, 22
—— Ironside, 23, 60
——, St, 94
Edred, King, 22
Edward (The Confessor), King, 23, 67
——, (The Elder), King, 22, 89
——, (The Martyr), King, 22
—— II, King, 84
—— III, King, 47, 84
—— IV, King, 26
Edwy, King, 22
Elite Hybrids Ltd, 123
Elizabeth I, Queen, 15, 27, 63, 65, 67, 75, 91-2
—— II, Queen, 92-3
Elliott, George, 92
Elmstead, 144

Elsenham, 126-7
Elsenham Quality Foods Ltd, 126-7
Englemann's Nursery, 161
Engineering, 139-45
English Electric Valve Co. Ltd, 141-2
Environment, Department of the, 76
Epping, 95, 150, 152, 156, 168
Epping Forest, 19-20, 31, 66, 95-6, 153-4, 163, 168, 168, 173
Epping Forest Conservation Centre, 153-4
Epping Street, 96
Epping Upland, 96
Eringo root, 155
Essex, Earls of, 25-6, 63, 83-4, 87
Essex Agricultural Society, 123, 133
—— Archaeological Society, 31, 168
—— Bird Report, 151
—— Bird-Watching and Preservation Society, 66, 151
—— Chronicle, The, 72
—— Countryside, 143, 170
—— County Council, 57, 59-60, 69, 90, 105, 113, 131, 158, 167-9
—— County Cricket Club, 71, 174
—— County Show, 121-4, 133
—— emerald moth, 152-3
—— Farmers' Hunt, 173
—— Field Club, 31, 150-1, 171
—— Gliding Club, 175
—— Half Black pig, 122
—— Hunt, 173
—— Naturalists' Trust, 37, 40, 66, 149-51, 153-9
—— People 1750-1900, 38
—— Poets Group, 170
—— Record Office, 167-8, 174
—— Regiment, 31
—— Saddleback pig, 122
—— skipper butterfly, 152-3
—— Spice apple, 125
—— Union Hunt, 173
—— Way, 168
—— Young Farmer, 132
—— Youth Orchestra, 104, 169
—— and Suffolk Gliding Club, 175
—— and Suffolk Hunt, 173
Ethelred II, King, 22-3

Fairfax, General, 28, 73
Farrell, Gordon, 173
Faulkbourne Hall, 15
Feering, 54, 89-90
Felix Hall, Kelvedon, 122

Felstar wines, 129
Felsted, 17, 56, 117, 119, 129
Field Studies Council, 154
Finchingfield, 54, 85
Fingringhoe, 53, 66
Fingringhoe Wick, 154-5, 158
Fishing, 173
Fitzlewes, 26
FitzPeter, Geoffrey, 84
FitzWimarc, Robert, 67
Flatford Lock, 52
Flint, 12-13
Flitch Trial, 56
Flora of Essex, 149, 162
Flour-milling, 135
Flower Clubs, 171
Football, Association, 175
Football, Rugby, 175
Footwear, 138-9
Ford Company, 89, 108, 110, 142
Forest Way, 168
Forestry Commission, 130-1, 161
Forster, E. M., 54
Forty-five rebellion, the, 29
Foulness Island, 43-4, 61-2, 157
Friends, Society of, 29, 37, 75, 149-50
Friends of Essex Poets, the, 170
Friends of Friendless Churches, the, 54
Friends of Histroic Essex, the, 167
Friern Manor, 59
Friesian, British, 120-1, 131
Frink, Elisabeth, 105
Frinton & Walton U.D.C., 158
Frinton-on-Sea, 38, 140, 174
Fruit-growing, 125-7
Fryatt, Captain Charles Algernon, 36
Fyfield, 64, 159

Garden nature reserves, 159
Gardeners' Chronicle, 156
Gardening bodies, 171
GEC Diesels Ltd, 144
GEC-Marconi Electronics Ltd, 141
George II, King, 29
—— III, King, 62
—— IV, King, 45
Georgian period, 29-30, 78-9
Gestingthorpe, 14
Gibberd, Sir Frederick, 98
Gibson, George Stacey, 149
——, Wyatt George, 149
Gilbey, Sir Walter, 126
Gilders, Edwin, 39

Glasshouses, 127
Glegg, W. E. 150-1
Gliding, 175
Gloucester, Duke of, 84
Goldhanger, 125, 142-3
Golf, 112, 174
Good Easter, 56
Goodman, Lord, 111
Gosbecks, 21, 73
Gasfield lake, 173, 175
Grahame, Major Iain, 165-6
Grasses, 119
Gray, Charles, 78
Grays, 136
Great, Samuel, 155
—— Baddow, 141
—— Bardfield, 53-4, 156
—— Bentley, 122
—— Burstead, 91
—— Canfield, 24, 62-3
—— Chalvedon Hall, 114
—— Chesterford, 12, 88-9
—— Clacton, 39
—— Dunmow, 31, 56, 85
—— Easton, 56
—— Hallingbury, 67
—— Holland, 38, 121
—— Leighs, 133
—— Oakley, 36-7
—— Parndon Wood, 158
—— Sampford, 53
—— Stambridge, 62
—— Tey, 66
—— Wakering, 62
—— Waltham, 56, 129
—— Yeldham, 52
—— Eastern Railway Company, 35-6, 39
Greensted, 15, 93-5
Grey, Josian, 35
——, Richard, 35
Greyhound racing, 174
Griffin, Sir John Griffin, 88
Guernsey cattle, 121
Gulbenkian Foundation, 104
Gunfleet, the, 28
Guthrum, 21
Gypsy, HMS, 32

Hadfield, Miles, 161
Hadleigh, 46-8
Haestern, 44
Hales Wood, 157
Hallam, Arthur, 96

Halstead, 25, 52-3, 137, 163
Hamford Water Site, 37
Hammond Organ Society, 169
Hampden, Sir John, 65
Hampshire Down sheep, 124
Hanningfield Reservoir, 54, 130-1
Hardacnut, 23
Hare-hunting, 173-4
Harlow, 67-8, 98-107, 115, 135, 138, 175-6
—— Art Trust, 104
—— Arts Council, 170
—— Ballet Club, 104
—— Bowmen, 175
—— Choral Society, 104
—— Cycling Club, 176
—— Development Corporation, 98, 103
—— District Council, 158
—— Industrial Health Service, 106-7
—— Museum, 101
—— Organ Club, 168
—— Photographic Society, 105
—— Society of Art, 105
—— Symphony Orchestra, 104
—— Youth Orchestra, 104
—— and District Sports Trust, 103
—— and District Wildlife Society, 171
Harold I, King, 23
—— II, King, 23
Harris, John, 125
Hartford End, 56, 134-5
Harwich, 26, 28, 32-6, 52, 138, 173
—— Society, 34
Harwood, William, 152
Hastings, Battle of, 23-4
Hatfield Broad Oak, 25, 27
Hatfield Forest, 154, 162-3, 168, 173
—— Peverel, 58, 89
Havengore, 44, 62
Hawkwood, Sir John, 52
Helena, St, 80
Hempstead, 12
Henry I, King, 75, 83
—— II, King, 25
—— III, King, 47, 93
—— VII, King, 26
—— VIII, King, 15, 26-7, 57, 61, 63, 76, 87, 89, 93
—— Doubleday Research Association, 162-3
Hepworth, Barbara, 105
Herball, Turner's, 150
Hereford cattle, 121
Hester, Frederick, 49
Heybridge, 55, 143

Hicks, Charles, 38
Higbed, Thomas, 91
High Beach, 31, 96, 153
—— Easter, 56
—— Laver, 94
—— Ongar, 64
—— Roding, 17, 63
Hills, Lawrence D., 162
Historia Insectorum, 151-2
—— Plantarum, 149
Hoare, Benjamin, 89
Hockey, 175
Hoffmann Works, Chelmsford, 139
Holiday Fellowship, 168
Holland-on-Sea, 38
Hollytrees, The, 78
Holst, Gustav, 86
Honey Wood, Halstead, 163
Honorius, Emperor, 73
Hope, Henry & Sons Ltd, 144
Horham Hall, 15
Hornbeam, 130
Hornchurch, 45-6
Horndon-on-the-Hill, 91
Horses, 133
Horsey Island, 37
Horticultural bodies, 171
Hospitallers, 17
Houses, timber-framed, 16-17
Howard, Lord, 87-8
Howe Street, 56
Hullbridge, 60
Humphrey, Edmund, 59
Hunt, R., & Co. Ltd, 143
Hunter, William, 92
Hunting, 173
Hurst (Seedsmen), 118-19
Hutton, 128-9
Hyklott, William, 60

Ilford Ltd, 147
Industry, 102, 110-11, 134-47
Ingatestone, 14, 57, 92, 167
Insects, 151-3, 159-60
International Distillers and Vintners, 135
Iron Age, 19-20
Ispania, Richard de, 85

Jam-making, 125-7
James I, King, 27, 67
—— II, King, 29
Jaywick Sands, 39-40
Jermyn, Stanley Thomas, 149-50, 158-9, 162

Jersey cattle, 121
John, King, 25, 46-7, 75, 84
John Poley Trust, 91
Johnson, John, 69-70
Johnstone, Mrs Pamela, 163
Jones, Christopher, 35-6
Josian, the, 35
'Jumbo' water tower, 74

Kelvedon, 19, 54, 89, 119, 122
Kemp family, 85
Kent, 49-50
Kersley, Leo, 104
Killigrews, 57
Kingsdon Hall, Harlow, 98
Kingsford Bridge Marsh Reserve, 66
Kingswood Squash Club, 112

Lamarsh, 165
Lambert, Maurice, 108
Landguard Point, 26, 28
Landace pigs, 123
Langdon Hills, 113
Langford, 54
Langham, 52
Langleys, 56
Lanvalei, William de, III, 75
Large White pigs, 122-3
Lawford, 13, 19
Layer Brook, 66
Layer Marney, 14
Lea, River, 68, 127
Leaden Roding, 63
Lee, River, 68, 127
Lee Valley Regional Park Authority, 68
Leez Priory, 27, 58
Leigh National Nature Reserve, 157-8
Leigh-on-Sea, 44
Leighs Priory, 27, 58
Lewis, Dr L. Elwyn, 64
Limousin cattle, 122
Lindisfarne, Bishop of, 42
Lindsell, 56
Linford, 19
Linnaeus, Carl, 153
Lisle, Sir George, 28, 77
Little Baddow, 29, 58, 154, 169
—— Bardfield, 53-4
—— Braxted, 54
—— Canfield, 62
—— Chesterford, 88
—— Coggeshall, 14, 17
—— Dunmow, 56

—— Easton, 26
—— Hadham Hall, 63
—— Hallingbury, 67
—— Holland, 38
—— Leighs, 58
—— Oakley, 36-7
—— Sampford, 53, 156
—— Stambridge Hall, 62
—— Wakering, 62
—— Waltham, 56
—— Warley, 31
—— Wigborough, 32
London, Maurice Bishop of, 69
Loughton, 19-20, 65-6
Lucas, Sir Charles, 27-8, 76-7
——, John, 27, 76
Lucerne, 119
Lupins, 119-20

Mackenzie, Sir Compton, 42
Maclean, Dr Alan, 152
Magna Carta, 47, 75, 84
Maize, 118-19
Maldon, 22, 24, 53, 55, 134, 136, 141, 174-5
Maldon Crystal Salt Company, 134
Malting, 118
Mammals, 153, 163-5
Mandevilles, de, 24-5, 83-4, 87
Manningtree, 90, 175
Manorial system, 25
Manuden, 67
Maplin Sands, 43-4, 157
Marconi organization, 140-2
Margaret Roding, 63-4
Margaretting, 57
Marian Reaction, 91-2
Maris Huntsman, 117
Marks Tey, 90
Martello towers, 29, 35, 39
Martin, Christopher, 90-1
Mary, Queen, 27, 91-2
Mathew, Gervase Frederick, 152
Maxey, William, 54
Mayflower, the, 35, 90-1
McWilliam, F. E., 105
Mechi, John Joseph, 126
Medway, River, 28
Mellitus, Bishop, 21
Merrett, Christopher, 150
Mersea Island, 22, 26, 41
Mesolithic period, 18
Mid-Essex Beagles, 173-4
Milton Hall (Southend) Brick Co., 136

Minories, The, 78-9, 169
Mistley, 118
Moats, 17
Mole Hall Wildlife Park, 163-4
Molehill Green, 58, 62
Montgomery, Sir John, 15
Moore, Henry, 104-5
Moot House Players, 104
Morgan, John D., 110-11
Morris dancing, 72, 86
Mountnessing, 16, 57
Mundon, 129
Munnings, Sir Alfred, 135
Murray Grey cattle, 122
Music, 104, 111, 168-9
Myson group, 139-40

Napoleonic Wars, 29-30, 35, 38-9, 43, 79
National Artillery Association, 44
—— Cactus and Succulent Society, 171
—— Seed Development Organization, 117
—— Trust, 154
—— Youth Orchestra, 104
Nature, 148-66
—— Conservancy Council, 37, 113, 157-8
Navestock, 16
Naze, the, 37, 155-6, 158
Neolithic period, 18-19
Nesfield, Eden, 53
Netteswell Players, 104
Nevendon Hall, 115
New England, 44, 62
New Hall vineyard, 129
'New Southend', 45
Neylan, Michael, 100
Noel, Conrad, 86
——, Miriam, 86
Nonconformists, 29
Norcros group, 143
Norden, John, 116
Norfolk, Fourth Duke of, 87
Norman Essex, 24-5, 83, 129
Normandy, William Duke of, 23
North Fambridge, 60
—— Weald, 175
—— Essex Foot Beagles, 174
Northey Island, 53
Norton Heath, 158
Norwich, Earl of, 28
Nuffield Provincial Hospitals Trust, 106

Oates, Titus, 29
Oats, 118

O'Brien (the giant), 95
Oil industry, 145
Old Harlow, 98-100, 173
Old Peoples' Clubs, 105-6
O'Leary, Patrick, 109
Ongar, 30, 64, 95, 140
Orwell, River, 26, 52
Othona, 21, 42-3
Oxford, Earls of, 26, 52, 53, 55
Oysters, 41-2

Paglesham, 62
Paine, John, 92
Palmer, Thomas, 96
Pant, River, 53-4
Pargetting, 53
Parkeston Quay, 34
Parnell, James, 75
Paschal II, Pope, 76
Paxman Diesels Ltd, 144
Paycocks, 54
Peasants' Revolt, 26
Pebble rubble, 13
Perfumes, 146
Pertwee, Rev. Arthur, 40-1
Petre family, 29-30, 57, 92
Pett, Peter, 35
Pevsner, Sir Nikolaus, 15, 41, 61, 78, 149
Photographic film, 147
Pigs, 122-3
Pilgrim Fathers, 35-6, 90
Pitchbury Ramparts, 20
Plague, the Great, 29
Playhouse Co-operative Film Society, 105
Pleshey, 24, 83-4
Pliny, 89
Pods Brook, 54
Poetry, 170
Popish Plot, 29
Portsmouth, Elizabeth Countess of, 88
Potter, Tully, 170
Potter Street, 98
Potton, 44, 62
Poultry, 124-5
Power Sportshoes, 139
Prehistoric times, 18-19
Printing, 136, 152
Prittlewell, 45-6, 121
Protestants, burning of, 91-2
Pudding stone, 13
Purfleet, 136, 145
Purleigh, 55, 129
Putterill, Rev. Jack, 86

Quakers, 29, 37, 39, 75, 149-50

Radwinter, 53
Railways, 30, 32, 35, 45, 80
Ramblers' Association, 168
Ramsden Bellhouse, 59
Ramsden Crays, 59
Ramsey, 120
Ransome Hoffmann Pollard Ltd, 139
Raven, Charles, 148
Ray, Rev, Philip, 94
——, John, 148-9, 151-3
Rayleigh, 24, 129
Rayleigh, Lord, 120
Rayne Hall, 63
Rayon-making, 137
Rebow, Sir Isaac, 77
——, John, 77
——, Mary, 82
Red hills, 43
Redundant Churches Fund, 158
Rettendon, 59
Rich, Lord, 27, 58, 61-2
Richard I, King, 46, 84
—— II, King, 26, 84
—— III, King, 26
Ridley, T. D. & Sons (Brewers) Ltd, 134-5
Rie, Eudo de, 75
Ring Hill, 20
River Stour Trust, 52
Roach, River, 61-2
Robin, Jean, 161
Rochford, 19, 45, 61
Rodin, Auguste, 105
Roding, River, 62-6
Rodings, the, 63-4
Rodney, Admiral Lord, 128
Roman Catholics, 29-30, 57, 75, 80, 92
—— brick, 13-14, 23
—— Conquest, 20
—— Essex, 53, 88-90
—— River, 66, 73
Rookwood Hall, 63
Roses, 127-9
Roses, Wars of the, 26
Rothmans International, 146
Round, Colonel J. G., 130
——, J. Horace, 24
Rowney Wood, 55
Rowntree, Fred, 150
Royal Agricultural Benevolent Institution, 126
—— Agricultural College, 126

—— Burnham Yacht Club, 61
—— Corinthian Yacht Club, 61
—— National Rose Society, 128
Roydon, 68
Rubber sheeting, synthetic, 145-6
Ruggles family, 85
Ruggles-Brise family, 85-6
Rushley, 44, 62
Rye, 118

St Osyth, 12-13, 29, 40, 93, 161
St Osyth Bird-watching and Protection Club, 171
Saffron Walden, 12, 25, 53, 65, 87-8, 149, 161, 168-9
Sail Craft, Brightlingsea, 136
Saling, 160
Salt production, 43, 134
Salvation Army, 47-8, 81
Sawbridgeworth Marsh Nature Reserve, 158
Saxons, 21
Scarfe, Norman, 37
'Scotch colony', 30
Scott, George Gilbert, 31
Sculpture in Harlow, 104
Sea-angling, 173
Sedge, Robert, 57
Seeds, small, 119
Selo Ltd, 147
Septaria, 13, 34, 74
Seven Year War, 20
Shalford, 54
Sheep, 39-40, 43, 91, 123-4
Sheepen, 73
Shellhaven, 145
Shelton, Harold, 51
Shenfield, 169
Shoebury, 22
Shoeburyness, 44
Shopland herd, 121
Shrapnel, General, 43
Sible Hedingham, 52
Siege, Colchester, 16, 27, 29, 76-7
Sigebert the Good, King, 42
Silk industry, 30, 136-7
Silver End, 143-4
Simmental cattle, 122
Skipper's Island, 37
Smith, Sir Thomas, 65
——, Donald, 63
Southchurch, 46
Southend-on-Sea, 30, 44-6, 54-5, 136, 157-8, 168, 173-5

South Fambridge, 60
—— Shoebury, 46
—— Woodham Ferrers, 59-60
—— Essex Natural History Society, 171
Spong & Co. Ltd, 147
Sport, 71, 103, 111-13, 172-6
Springfield, 56-7
Spurgeon, C. H., 54, 80
Stambourne, 129
Standard Telephones & Cables Ltd, 142
Stane Street, 62, 90
Stansted Mountfitchet, 67
Stanway Hall, 66, 164-5
Stapleford Abbots, 64-5
Stapleford Tawney, 64-5
Stebbing, 58, 129
Stebbing Brook, 56
Steeple, 61
Steeple Bumpstead, 52
Stephen, King, 83
Stewart, Prince Charles Edward, 29
Stisted, 54
Stock, 90, 162
Stort, River, 67-8
Stour, River, 26, 51-2, 135
Strachan, Sir Richard, 36
Stratford St Mary, 52
Strode, the, 41
Strutt, Hon. Edward Gerald, 120
Sudbury, 52
Suffolk, Earls of, 87-8
—— horse, 133
—— sheep, 124
Sugar beet, 59, 119
Sussex, Earl of, 89
Sussman, L. S. & J. Ltd, 138
Sutton, 62
Sweet corn, 119
Sweyn, 22-4
Systema Naturae, 153

Taylor, John, 95
Templars, 17
Tendring, 122,
Tennis, 174
Tennyson, Alfred Lord, 96
Ter, River, 58
Terling, 58, 120
Textiles, 136-8
Thames, River, 26, 28, 47-9, 62, 66, 68, 113,
    136, 145, 156
Thaxted, 13, 15, 25, 29, 56, 86-7, 146, 169
Theatre, amateur, 170

Thermos Ltd, 146-7
Theydon Mount, 65
Thomas, Edward Boaden, 170
——, Stanley J., 170
Thompson, Arthur, 153
Thornton, Marianne, 54
Thorpe-le-Soken, 37
Thundersley, 173
Thurrock, 91, 136
Thurrock Natural History Society, 171
Tilbury, 26, 30, 92-3
Tile-making, 135-6
Tillingham, 43
Tilty, 56
Tiptree, 125-7, 152
Tofig (Tovi) the Proud, 23
Togodumnus, 20
Tollesbury, 125, 151
Tolleshunt D'Arcy, 125
Tolpuddle Martyrs, 94
Toppesfield, 129
'Tornado' catamarans, 136
Townswomen's Guilds, 172
Tractor production, 142
Treble, R., 112
Trees, 130-1, 160-2
Trinity House, 34, 37
Trinovantes, 19-20
Turkeys, 124-5
Turner, William, 150
Twedye, Richard, 90
Twitt, Sarah, 35
Tye Green, 100

Ulting, 58-9
United Hospitals' Sailing Club, 61
University of Essex, 82

Vacuum vessels, 146-7
Vallus, the, 89
Vange, 165
Vanson, Frederic, 170
Vegetables, 127
Vares, the de, 24-6, 52-3, 55
Vermuyden, Sir Cornelius, 48
Victoria, Queen, 30-1, 36, 80
Vine cultivation, 129

Waad family, 67
Wakes Colne, 53
Walcheren expedition, 36
Walden Forest, 163
Walker, Dr Anthony, 64

Wallasea, 44, 61-2
Wallbury Camp, 20, 67-8
Waltham Abbey, 23, 68, 96
Waltham Abbey Historical Society, 168
—— Holy Cross, 23, 68, 96
Walton, Izaak, 68
Walton-on-the-Naze, 18, 29, 37, 39, 173
Warley Rose Gardens, 128-9
Washington, Laurence, 55
Water skiing, 175
Watts-Ditchfield, John Edwin, 71
Weavers, Protestant, 27
Wegg, George, 79
West Hanningfield, 15
—— Horndon, 26
—— Mersea, 41
—— Tilbury, 21, 42
Western, Baron, 122
Wethersfield, 54
Wheat, 117-18
White, Colne, 19
——, Roding, 63
Wickford, 59, 136
Wickham Bishops, 54
Wid, River, 56-7
Widdington, 163
Widford, 57
Wilhelm II, Kaiser, 36
Wilkin & Sons Ltd, 125-7

William I, King, 23-4, 67, 75, 83
—— II, King, 75
Williams, Ben, & Co. Ltd, 138
Willow growing, 130
Wimbish, 53
'Windmill land', 63
Wine production, 129
Winsley, Arthur, 77
Wiseman family, 62-3
Witham, 12, 19, 22, 89, 118, 136, 143
Witham Natural History Society, 171
Wivenhoe, 53, 66, 82
Women's Institutes, 172
Wood, Marguerite, 170
——, Thomas, 92
Woodham Fen, 60, 158
Woodstock, Thomas of, 84
World Pheasant Association, 165-6
Writtle, 57, 131, 141
—— Agricultural College, 131-2

Yardley, 110-11, 146
York, Duke of, 29
Young, Arthur, 85
—— Pretender, 29
—— Farmers' Clubs, 132-3
Youth Opera Basildon Area (YOBA), 169

Zeppelins, 32